the right-handed *embroiderer's* companion

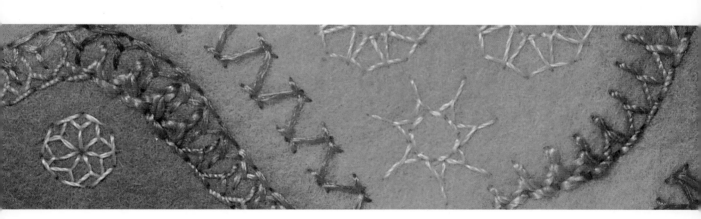

Published by Vetty Creations.
PO Box 1723, Hornsby Westfield NSW 1635, Australia
Copyright © Yvette Stanton 2010.
Reprinted 2010, 2011.

www.vettycreations.com.au

**The National Library of Australia
Cataloguing-in-Publication data**

Stanton, Yvette. 1974—
    The right-handed embroiderer's companion: a step-by-step stitch dictionary

    160 p. : col. ill ; 28 cm
    Bibliography.
    Includes index.
    ISBN 9780975767740 (pbk.).

    1. Stitches (Sewing) 2. Embroidery – Handbooks, manuals, etc. 3. Needlework – Handbooks, manuals, etc. II. Title

746.44

Book design: Yvette Stanton, Vetty Creations
Printed in China

other books by yvette stanton

*The Left-Handed Embroiderer's Companion:
    a Step-by-Step Stitch Dictionary*
Elegant Hardanger Embroidery
*Ukrainian Drawn Thread Embroidery: Merezhka
    Poltavska*
and with Prue Scott:
Mountmellick Embroidery: Inspired by Nature

dedication
For Emma.

acknowledgments
Thanks to my family who are always supportive of my creative pursuits. Thanks also to the right-handed embroiderers who felt left out when I published my left-handed stitch dictionary, because you prompted me to do this right-handed version.

    Thanks to God who gifted me with my creativity in the first place. My aim is to glorify Him in all that I do.

selected bibliography/further reading
Bauer, Margie. *A-Z of Embroidery Stitches.* Country Bumpkin Publications, Malvern SA. 1997

Butler, Anne. *The Batsford Encyclopaedia of Embroidery Stitches.* BT Batsford, London. 1979

Conrad, Leon. "A Treatise on Plaited Braid Stitch Part 1" *Finelines.* Vol 8, No 1

de Dillmont, Thérèse. *The Complete Encyclopedia of Needlework.* 4th ed. Running Press, Philadelphia Pennsylvania. 2002

Eaton, Jan. *The Complete Stitch Encyclopedia.* Hamlyn Publishing, Middlesex. 1986

Enthoven, Jacqueline. *The Stitches of Creative Embroidery.* Schiffer Publishing Ltd, Atglen PA. 1987

Howard, Constance. *The Constance Howard Book of Stitches.* B T Batsford, London. 1979

Nichols, Marion. *Encyclopedia of Embroidery Stitches, Including Crewel.* Dover Publications, New York. 1974

O'Connor, Susan. *A-Z of Embroidery Stitches 2.* Country Bumpkin Publications, Malvern SA. 2007

Reader's Digest Complete Guide to Needlecraft. Reader's Digest, Sydney. 1987

O'Steen, Darlene. *The Proper Stitch.* Rev ed. Hoffman Media, Alabama. 2006

Thomas, Mary. *Mary Thomas's Dictionary of Embroidery Stitches.* Hodder and Stoughton Ltd, London. 1934

Weldons Encyclopedia of Needlework. The Waverley Book Co, London. Undated

Wilson, Erica. *Erica Wilson's Embroidery Book.* Faber and Faber Ltd, London. 1973

the right-handed *embroiderer's* companion

YVETTE STANTON

a step-by-step stitch dictionary

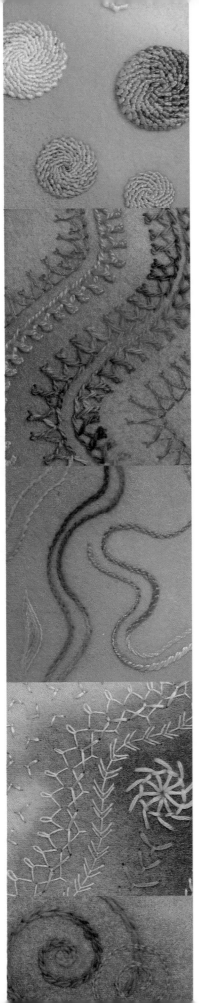

contents

introduction

The Right-Handed Embroiderer's Companion is twin to *The Left-Handed Embroiderer's Companion*. Following the success of that book, I found that there was a new condition called 'left-handed envy', because right-handed stitchers were jealous of the left-handers' stitch dictionary. We can't have that sort of unhappiness, so this new right-handed version aims to fix the balance.

Most stitches are shown with guide lines marked on the fabric. When you are learning a stitch on a sample piece, use guides drawn or stitched on your fabric. The more you practice the stitch, the less you will probably need these guide lines. However, if you do, make sure the lines are removable or completely coverable.

The stitches in this book are ordered so that the main stitches are in alphabetical order. Variations of these main stitches follow in rough order of complexity. If you're having trouble finding a stitch, use the index to locate it. The index also includes many alternate stitch names.

Each stitch has step-by-step instructions to lead the stitcher through the stitch process. Each step has a diagram to show what to do. All stitches have a photo of the finished stitch and a photo showing the stitch used in embroidery, to inspire creative use.

For each stitch, there is also a picture and a note explaining how left-handers would do the stitch, compared to right-handers. However, we highly recommend that left-handers use *The Left-Handed Embroiderer's Companion* instead of this book, as it is written specifically for left-handed embroiderers.

With *The Right-Handed Embroiderer's Companion* as your constant stitching companion, you will have clear step-by-step stitch instructions at your fingertips. Enjoy the new horizons it brings!

hand embroidery needles

Needles are an important part of an embroiderer's workbox. Keep them clean and dry. Storing them in your embroidery fabric can cause them to rust. Needles that are rusted, burred or have a flaking surface should be discarded as they will not pass cleanly through the fabric.

needle size

The needle makes a hole to enable the passage of the thread through the fabric. Ideally your needle should be the same thickness as the thread you are using when it is doubled over. This is because the doubled over thread near the eye is the thickest part to be pulled through.

Too narrow a needle, and the hole it creates will be too small, causing abrasion on the thread. When thread becomes furry and worn-looking very quickly, it is likely that the needle is too small. Too thick a needle and the hole may remain large after the needle and thread have passed through.

Needles are usually numbered so that the smaller numbers are for the larger needles e.g. a No 1 darner will be thicker than a No 5 darner needle.

The eye sizes of needles can change between brands, so the eye might be too small in one size of one brand, but suitable in another. If the eye is too small for the thread it will also cause extra wear and tear on the thread.

needle type

Embroidery or crewel needles are used for fine threads such as a few strands of embroidery floss, or fine wools. They are a good all-purpose embroidery needle. They have a relatively large eye which assists with threading.

Sharps are also a good general purpose embroidery needle. They have small eyes and are suited to embroidery with fine thread.

Tapestry and chenille needles are similar in most respects, however, tapestry needles have a rounded point while chenilles have a sharp point. Tapestry needles are used for tapestry, counted thread embroidery, and drawn and pulled thread work, as the rounded point enables them to pass cleanly between the fabric threads without splitting them. Chenille needles are used for wool, thick perle cottons or even silk ribbons. Their large eyes can be threaded easily.

Milliner or straw needles are used primarily for knotted stitches such as bullions knots. The thickness of the eye is similar to the rest of the shaft, allowing the threaded needle to pass through the knot's wraps with relative ease. Their long length allows for very long bullions to be made. For threads that are too thick for milliner needles, darners can be substituted.

Darner needles, also known as yarn or wool darners, are often used for sewing up woollen garments, but are useful for embroidery with thick threads.

Betweens or quilting needles are short, fine needles that are most often used for quilting as their short length enables very fast and even stitching.

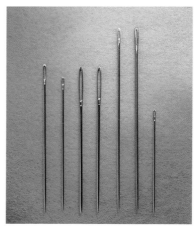

L-R: embroidery needle, sharp needle, tapestry needle, chenille needle, milliner needle, darner needle, between needle.

using the back end of a needle

Sometimes it would be helpful to have a sharp-ended needle to pierce the fabric, and a tapestry needle (with its blunt point) for sliding under stitches without catching them, for the one stitch. Changing between two needles constantly would slow down the process immensely. In these instances, when you need the blunt-ended needle, turn the sharp-ended needle around and use the blunt, eye end instead.

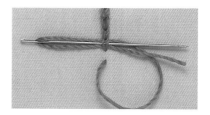

starting a thread

There are a number of methods for starting a new thread. Do not carry threads over long distances on the back of the work. This can cause puckering and be prone to snagging, or show through obviously when framed. Finish the thread and start anew.

anchoring in existing stitching

When there is already existing stitching nearby, you can anchor the thread in the back of that stitching.

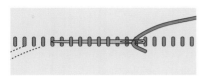

1 On the back of the fabric, run the thread under the back of nearby stitching.

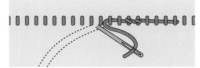

2 Take a small back stitch or two into the back of the stitching. Take the thread to the front at the desired location and begin stitching.

knots

A knotted thread should only be used when the lump on the fabric back (caused by the knot) will not show through to the front.

Tie a neat knot in the thread end, bring the needle to the front in the desired location, and begin stitching.

Knots should never be used on work to be framed. They could also come undone, or slip through to the fabric front, becoming useless.

split back stitch

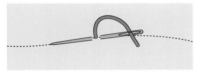

1 On the front, bring the thread out where it will be covered by stitching. Take a tiny back stitch.

2 Work another tiny back stitch into the first, splitting the first one.

3 Work another back stitch to split the previous one. Tug sharply to test that it holds well. Begin stitching over the top of it.

waste knot

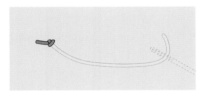

1 Make a knot in the end of the thread. From the front of the fabric, enter the needle about 8 cm (3 in) away from the start of the stitching.

2 Begin stitching. When there is enough length to run a thread through the back, cut off the knot.

3 On the back of the fabric, run the thread under the back of the stitching. A back stitch will help to further anchor it. Trim any excess thread.

finishing a thread

To finish a thread, take it through to the back and run it under the back of the stitching, adding a few back stitches to help secure the thread.

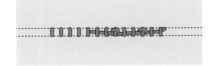

antwerp edging stitch

This stitch makes an attractive knotted edging and is best worked in a thick thread. Also known as *knot stitch* and *knotted blanket stitch*. It can be worked to actually hem the edge, or the edge can be hemmed then the edging stitch worked separately as a decoration.

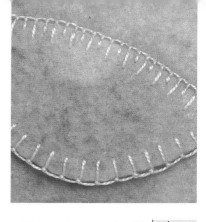

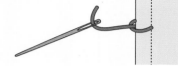

1 Use one guide line close to the folded fabric edge. Bring the needle out through the edge of the fold.

2 Just below, insert the needle into the line, bringing it out under the fabric edge. Take the thread under the needle point.

3 Pull the needle through to form a loose blanket stitch.

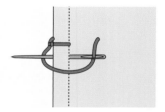

4 Insert the needle from right to left into the blanket stitch and under the thread emerging from it. Take the thread under the needle point.

5 Pull the needle through to create a neat knot.

6 Using longer spacing than before, insert the needle into the line. Bring it out under the fabric edge. Take the thread under the needle point.

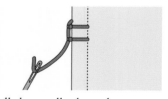

7 Pull the needle through to form a loose blanket stitch.

8 Insert the needle from right to left into the blanket stitch and under the thread emerging from it. Take the thread under the needle point.

9 Pull the needle through to create a neat knot.

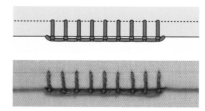

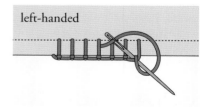

left-handed

10 Using the same spacing as for the last stitch, continue stitching.

11 To finish, take the needle into the fabric edge, a short distance from the final stitch. Turn the work 90 degrees anticlockwise for the final effect.

❶ *Left-handers work this stitch from left to right, turned 90 degrees anticlockwise.*

armenian edging stitch

This firm knotted edge can be worked to actually hem the edge, or the edge can be hemmed then the edging stitch worked separately as a decoration.

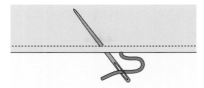

1 Use one guide, close to the folded edge of the hem. Bring the thread out at the edge. Insert the needle in the back of the hem, bringing it out on the line, a little way to the left.

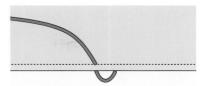

2 Pull the needle through, and leave the stitch hanging down in a gentle loop.

3 With the needle pointing to the edge, insert the needle tip into the loop, over the thread.

4 Move the needle to the right, and bring the needle point up over the edge of the fabric, right of where the thread emerged from it.

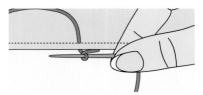

5 Keeping the loop on the needle, swing the eye of the needle up to the right, so that the needle points to the left.

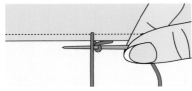

6 Where the thread emerges from the fabric, bring it down in front of the needle.

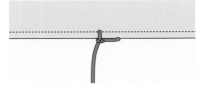

7 Pull the needle through, and tighten the resulting knot.

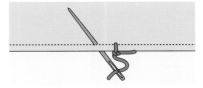

8 Using the same spacing as before, insert the needle in the back of the hem, bringing it out on the line, a little way left.

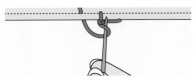

9 Pull the needle through so the stitch hangs down in a loop. Insert the needle as before, moving it right, then bringing the needle point up over the edge of the fabric, right of the previous knot.

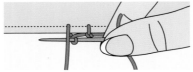

10 Keeping the loop on the needle, swing the eye of the needle up to the right, so that the needle points to the left. Where the thread emerges from the fabric, bring it down in front of the needle.

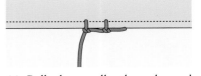

11 Pull the needle through, and tighten the resulting knot.

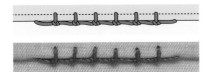

12 Continue in the same way to build up a line of stitching. To finish, take the thread into the edge of the hem fold, and fasten on the back.

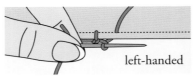

left-handed

❶ *Left-handers work this stitch in mirror image, from left to right.*

back stitch

Back stitch is also known as *point de sable* and *stitching*. It is the finest solid linear stitch that can be made, and is very useful for outlining.

1 Use one guide. Bring the thread out on the line a stitch length to the left of where the stitched line needs to begin.

2 Insert the needle a stitch length to the right. Bring the needle out again one stitch length to the left of where the thread first emerged.
❶ *The stitch goes 'back' to the start.*

3 Pull the needle through so that the stitch lies flat on the fabric surface.

4 Insert the needle in the same hole as the end of the previous stitch. Bring the needle out again the same distance to the left of the emerging thread.
❶ *Each stitch on top of the fabric goes 'back' to meet the previous one.*

5 Repeat to build up a line of stitching.

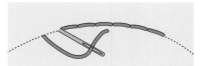

6 To finish, insert the needle back at the end of the previous stitch. Pull the thread through so that the final stitch lies flat.

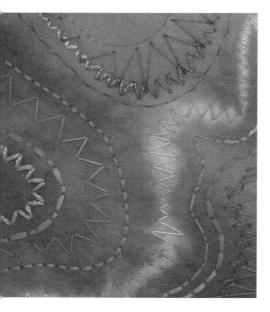

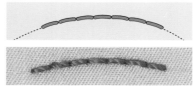

7 The finished back stitch.

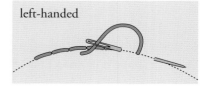

left-handed

❶ *Left-handers work this stitch in mirror image, from left to right.*

zigzagging back stitch

1 Use two lines. Bring the needle out on the lower line. From the right, make a stitch in the top line, so the stitch's centre sits above the emerging thread.

2 Pull the needle through. Using the same stitch length as before, make a stitch in the lower line starting at the end of the first stitch.

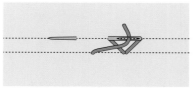

3 Pull the needle through. Make a stitch in the upper line from the end of the previous stitch.

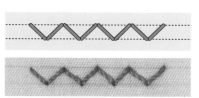

4 Continue making stitches in alternate lines to build up a line of stitches.

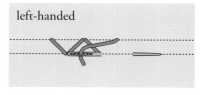

left-handed

❶ *Left-handers work this stitch in mirror image, from left to right.*

double back stitch

On transparent fabric, this stitch, also known as *shadow work*, creates a shadow effect through the fabric. Use very short stitches for better coverage and more colour showing through.

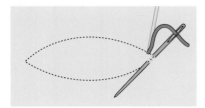

1 Begin with a waste knot. Bring the needle out on the upper line a stitch length away from the right end. Insert the needle back in the right end point. Bring it out again on the lower line, a stitch length along.

❶ *For best results, use short stitches: 1.5–2mm (¹/₁₀–¹/₈in) or less.*

2 Pull the needle through. Insert the needle back in the point. Bring it out on the upper line, a stitch length from the end of the first stitch.

❶ *It is called double back stitch, as two lines of back stitch are worked simultaneously.*

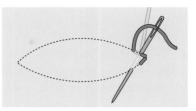

3 Pull the needle through. Insert the needle right at the end of the previous stitch in the upper line. Bring the needle out a stitch length further along on the lower line.

❶ *A pattern of herringbone forms on the reverse of the fabric.*

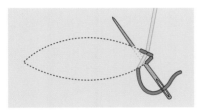

4 Pull the needle through. Insert the needle right at the end of the lower line's previous stitch. Bring the needle out further along on the upper line.

5 Pull the needle through. Insert the needle right at the end of the upper line's previous stitch. Bring the needle out further along on the lower line.

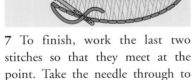

6 Continue working in the same way, to the far end of the shape.

7 To finish, work the last two stitches so that they meet at the point. Take the needle through to the back.

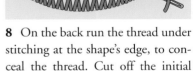

8 On the back run the thread under stitching at the shape's edge, to conceal the thread. Cut off the initial waste knot and fasten it similarly.

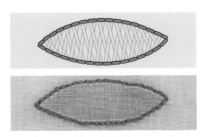

9 The completed shadow work.

❶ *For curves, alter the stitch length so the stitches stay roughly opposite each other. Inner curves need shorter stitches, outer curves need longer.*

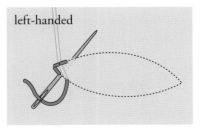

left-handed

❶ *Left-handers work this stitch in mirror image.*

threaded back stitch
The threading can be in the same or a contrasting colour.

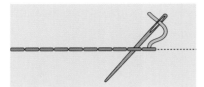

1 Work a line of back stitch. Using a tapestry needle, bring a new thread out from under the top of the right-most stitch. Without entering the fabric, slide the needle under the next stitch, from above.

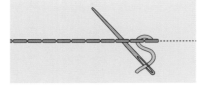

2 Pull the needle through. Slide the needle under the next back stitch from below.
❶ *Do not enter the fabric.*
❶ *Do not pull the thread too tight or the stitch will disappear.*

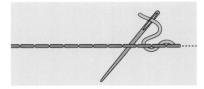

3 Pull the needle through. Slide the needle under the next stitch from above.
❶ *Do not enter the fabric.*

4 Continue in the same way. To finish, take the thread to the back under the centre of the last back stitch.

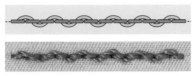

5 The finished threaded back stitch.

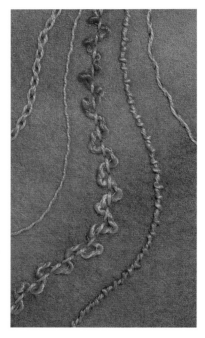

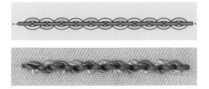

❶ *Back stitch can be double threaded, with additional stitching worked in the gaps between the first threading.*

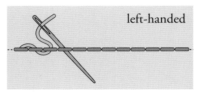

left-handed

❶ *Left-handers work in mirror image, starting at the left end and working right.*

whipped back stitch

1 Work a line of back stitch. Using a tapestry needle, bring the new thread out from under the top of the first stitch on the right.

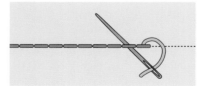

2 Slide the needle under the next back stitch along, from below.
❶ *Do not enter the fabric.*

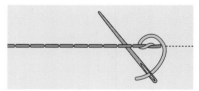

3 Pull the needle through. Slide the needle under the next stitch, from below.
❶ *Do not enter the fabric.*

4 Continue in the same way. To finish, take the thread to the back under the centre of the last back stitch.

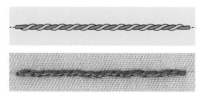

5 The finished whipped back stitch.

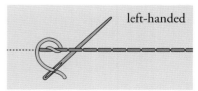

left-handed

❶ *Left-handers work this stitch in mirror image, from the left end.*

pekinese stitch

Pekinese stitch is an interlaced back stitch. The lacing can be worked in the same colour as the back stitch or a contrasting colour. In historical Chinese embroidery, Pekinese stitch is used both as a linear stitch and a filling stitch.

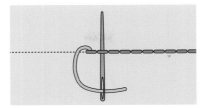

1 Work a line of back stitch. With a tapestry needle, bring a new thread out from under the top of the leftmost stitch. Without entering the fabric, slide the needle under the second stitch, from below.

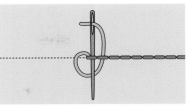

2 Pull the needle through, but do not tighten the stitch yet. Without entering the fabric, slide the needle under the first stitch, from above. Take the needle over the looped thread.

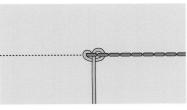

3 Pull the thread leading to the needle eye upwards through the stitches, then pull the needle down and through. Do not tighten too much, but leave the stitches looping gently.

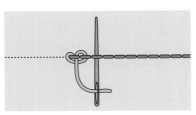

4 Slide the needle under the next back stitch, from below.

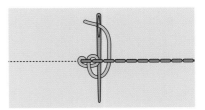

5 Pull the needle through, but do not tighten the stitch yet. Slide the needle under the previous back stitch, from above. Take the needle over the looped thread.

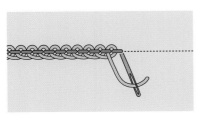

6 Continue in the same manner. To finish, take the thread to the back at the end of the back stitching.

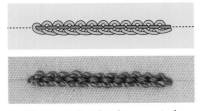

7 The completed Pekinese stitch.

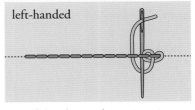

left-handed

❶ *Left-handers work in mirror image from right to left.*

pekinese stitch variation

This variation is worked through parallel lines of back stitch.

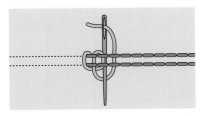

1 Work two lines of back stitch, where pairs of stitches align, as a foundation for the stitching. Work as for regular Pekinese stitch, but through the two lines together.

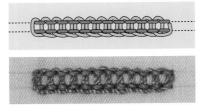

2 The completed variation.

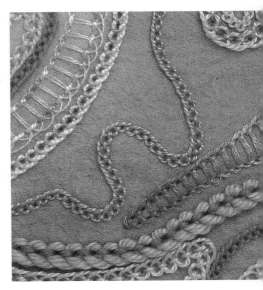

double pekinese stitch

Double Pekinese stitch uses a foundation of two lines of back stitch. A new thread is laced between and through the foundation.

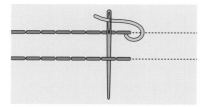

1 Work two lines of back stitch, where pairs of stitches align. Bring the thread out from underneath the lower side of the first stitch from the right end in the upper row. Slide the needle from above under the second stitch in the lower row.

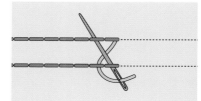

2 Pull the needle through. From below, slide the needle under the first stitch from the right end in the lower row, over the laced thread and under the second stitch in the upper row.
❶ *The needle goes over the laced stitch.*

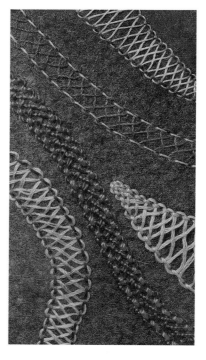

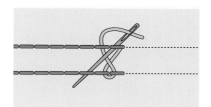

3 Pull the needle through. From above, slide the needle under the first stitch in the upper row, over the laced thread and under the third stitch in the lower row.
❶ *The needle goes over the laced stitch.*

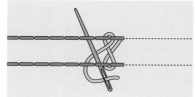

4 Pull the needle through. From below, slide the needle under the second stitch in the lower row, over the laced thread and under the third stitch in the upper row.
❶ *The needle goes over the laced stitch.*

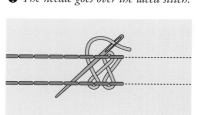

5 Pull the needle through. From above, slide the needle, under the second stitch in the upper row, over the laced thread and under the fourth stitch in the lower row.
❶ *The needle goes over the laced stitch.*

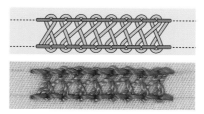

6 Continue in the same way to build up a line of stitching. To finish, take the thread through to the back under the final back stitch.

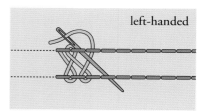

left-handed

❶ *Left-handers work this stitch in mirror image, from left to right.*

basque stitch

Basque stitch comes from the Basque region in northern Spain. It is traditionally worked in white thread on blue fabric, or red thread on green fabric.

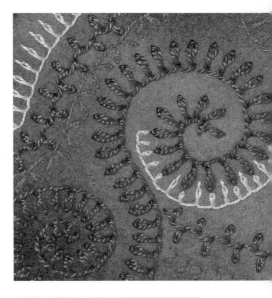

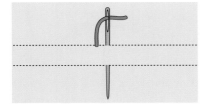

1 Use two guides. Bring the thread out on the top line. A short way to the right, vertically insert the needle from the top to the bottom line.

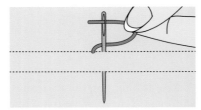

2 Take the thread leading to the needle eye, towards the right behind the upper part of the needle.

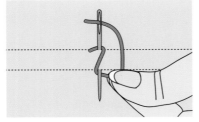

3 Take the thread down and around to the left of the needle point.

4 Take the thread to the right, behind the needle point.

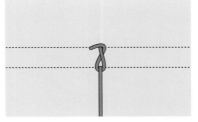

5 Pull the needle through to create a twisted chain stitch with a 'curved top' at the top.

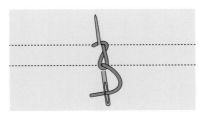

6 Insert the needle just below the lowest part of the loop, bringing it out near the top of the twisted chain, just below the 'curved top'.

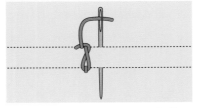

7 Using the same spacing as before, vertically insert the needle from the top line to the bottom line.

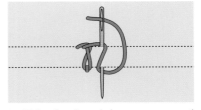

8 Take the thread down, across and around the needle point as before.

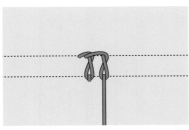

9 Pull the needle through to tighten the twisted chain.

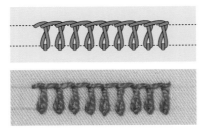

10 Continue in the same way, to build up a line of stitching. To finish, take a short stitch over the base of the last basque stitch.

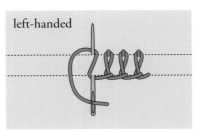

left-handed

❶ *Left-handers work this stitch turned 180 degrees, with the twisted chains at the top, travelling from right to left.*

15

braid edging stitch

This stitch makes a pretty hemmed edge. A thread with body will enable the loops to maintain their shape.

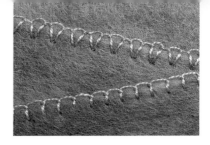

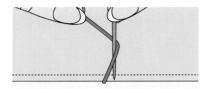

1 Use one guide close to the folded hem edge. Bring the thread out at the edge. With the thread in your left hand, place the needle across the thread. Move the needle right, taking the point under the thread near where it emerges from the hem.

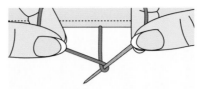

2 Maintaining the thread tension with your left hand, move the needle down past the edge of the hem.

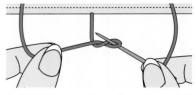

3 Maintaining thread tension with your left hand, move the needle point forward and up over the front of the twisted thread.

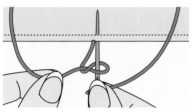

4 Insert the needle behind the hem, coming out on the line, just right of where the thread emerged.

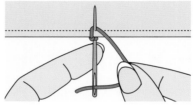

5 Using a finger to steady the needle, take the thread under the needle point and down to the right with your right hand. Tighten the thread around the needle so that it is snug.

6 Pull the needle through the fabric and strongly downwards to tighten the knot on the back of the fabric.

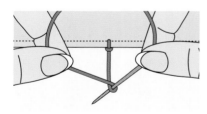

7 Make a wrap around the needle as before.

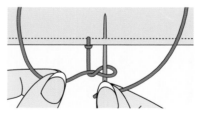

8 Bringing the needle point up over the front of the twisted threads, insert it behind the hem, coming out on the line, a little to the right of the previous knot.

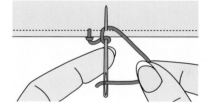

9 Take the thread up under the needle point and down to the right. Tighten the thread around the needle so that it is snug.

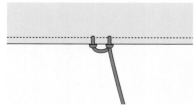

10 Pull the needle through the fabric and strongly downwards to tighten the knot on the back, creating a gentle loop between knots.

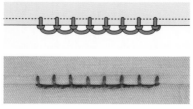

11 Continue in the same way to build up a line of stitching. To finish, take the thread into the hem right next to the final knot.

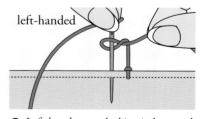

❶ *Left-handers work this stitch turned 180 degrees, with the loops at the top, from right to left.*

breton stitch

Breton stitch is similar to closed herringbone stitch, but with an extra twist in the cross-over sections. This stitch comes from Brittany in France.

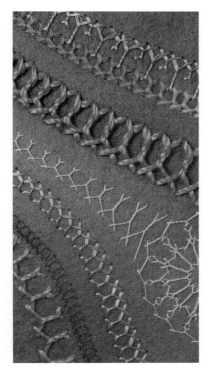

1 Use two guide lines. Bring the thread out on the lower line. In the top line, take a short stitch from right to left, finishing a little to the right of the emerging thread.

3 Pull the needle through, thus twisting the stitches together.

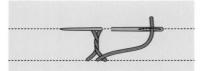

5 Pull the needle through. Take a stitch in the top line, from right to left, with the needle emerging in the same place as the top right part of the earlier stitch.

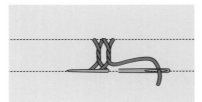

7 Pull the needle through, thus twisting the stitches together. Take a stitch in the lower line, so that the stitch touches the right 'leg' of the previous twisted stitch.

left-handed

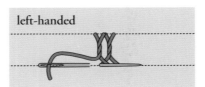

❶ *Left-handers work in mirror image, from right to left.*

2 Pull the needle through. From the right, slide the needle under the diagonal stitch, without entering the fabric.

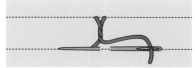

4 Using the same stitch length as before, take a stitch from right to left in the bottom line, finishing one stitch length right of where the thread originally emerged.

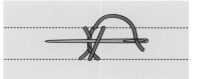

6 Pull the needle through. Slide the needle under the diagonal stitch, from right to left.
❶ *Do not enter the fabric.*

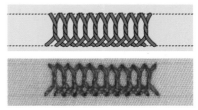

8 Continue in the same manner to build up a line of stitching.

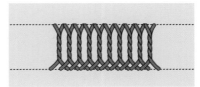

❶ *For taller stitches, the needle can be slid under the diagonal stitches twice, to create a double twist.*

17

bonnet stitch

Bonnet stitch was named after it was found as an unknown stitch on a bonnet in an old magazine. Similar in appearance to Breton stitch, it is worked quite differently.

1 Use two guides. Bring the thread out on the bottom line. A little to the left, take a short stitch from right to left on the top line. Take the thread under the needle point.

2 Pull the needle through, so that the working thread emerges from under the stitch.

3 Level with the first stitch's top end, insert the needle just above the bottom line and the first stitch's lower part. Bring it out to the left, below the line, with the thread under the needle point.

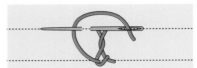

4 Pull the needle through. Using the same stitch length and spacing as before, take a stitch in the top line from right to left. Take the thread under the needle point.

5 Pull the needle through. Take a stitch from above the previous stitch, to just below the bottom line, using the spacing and stitch length as before. Take the thread under the needle point.

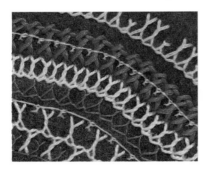

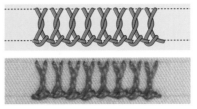

6 Continue in the same way to build up a line of stitching. To finish, take a short stitch over the final chain section.

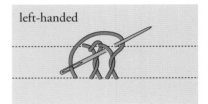

left-handed

❶ *Left-handers work this stitch turned 180 degrees.*

bullion knot

Also called *bullion stitch, caterpillar stitch, coil stitch, grub knot, knot stitch, Porto Rico rose, post stitch, roll stitch* and *worm stitch*.

1 Use a milliner's needle. Bring the thread out of the fabric. Insert the needle again some distance away.
❶ *A milliner's needle has a narrow eye which slides through the wraps easier.*

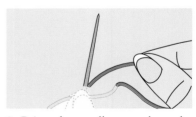

2 Bring the needle out where the thread first emerged. Pull it part way through, so that most of it is above the fabric. Hold the needle eye below the fabric with your left hand.

3 Wrap the thread around the needle three times in a clockwise direction.
❶ *Wrapping can be clockwise or anti-clockwise. Each produces a different result.*

4 Push the wraps down to the base of the needle to sit stacked against the fabric.

5 Wrap the thread clockwise around the needle a few more times.

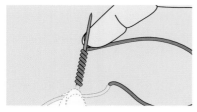

6 Push the wraps down again. Wrap as many times as are necessary to span the stitch length.

8 Continue to gently pull the thread through the wraps until they lie flat against the fabric.

bullions and thread twist

Wrapping in the opposite direction will create different results, because of the way the thread twists.

Most threads are 's' twist, meaning that they twist in a clockwise direction, when looking at the end of the thread. The remainder of threads are 'z' twist, which twist in an anticlockwise direction.

overwrapped bullions

Overwrapping makes curved bullions that sit up from the fabric surface or that can be couched to lay flat against it in their curved shape.

❶ *By gently stroking the threads in a clockwise direction the wraps will become tighter. Conversely, stroking in an anticlockwise direction will produce looser wraps, which can be useful when struggling to pull the needle through.*

9 Insert the needle into the fabric at the end of the bullion.

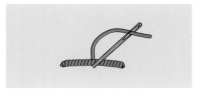

❶ *Very long bullions can be couched in order to hold the full length in place.*

For 's' twist threads, clockwise wrapping (above left) produces a smooth result, because the threads can untwist a little and the separate plies flatten out to wrap like a ribbon.

When wrapping anticlockwise (above right), the threads twist more, producing wraps that are tightly twisted and distinctly separate.

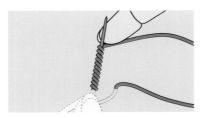

1 Create more wraps than are needed to span the stitch length.
❶ *The more wraps, the higher the bullion will sit up from the fabric.*

7 Loosely hold the wraps between your left thumb and forefinger. Gently pull the needle and thread through with your right hand.

10 Pull the thread through to the back to complete the bullion.

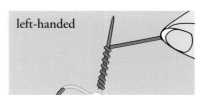

left-handed

❶ *Left-handed stitchers work this stitch in the same way.*

For 'z' twist threads, clockwise wrapping (above left) produces distinct wraps, and anticlockwise wrapping (above right) creates a smooth result.

2 Pull the needle through, and allow the bullion to sit up from the fabric rather than overtightening it to force the bullion to sit flat.

19

bullion loop

This stitch is a very overwrapped bullion, worked over a very short distance, creating a loop.

1 Bring the thread out of the fabric. Insert the needle one or two threads to the left. Then, leaving most of the thread at the front, take the needle through to the back.

2 Bring the needle point to the front where the thread originally emerged.
❶ *Do not bring the needle all the way through. Hold just the eye of the needle under the fabric with your left hand.*

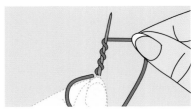

3 Take the right part of the thread loop in your right hand. Wrapping in a clockwise direction, wrap the thread around the needle three times.

4 Push the wraps down to the base of the needle with your finger.

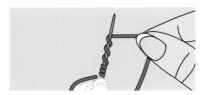

5 Wrap the thread clockwise around the needle a few more times.

6 Push the wraps down again. Wrap and stack as many times as is necessary for the desired number of wraps.

7 Loosely hold the wraps in place with your right hand. With your left, pull the needle through the wraps.
❶ *To slightly loosen the wraps, move your right thumb towards the right, and your right forefinger to the left.*

8 Pull the thread through so that the wraps tighten at the base of the bullion loop.

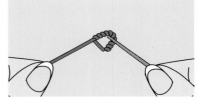

9 Temporarily place the needle point in the loop to hold it open. Pull the thread down to the left to gently continue tightening.

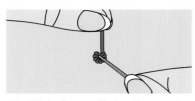

10 With the needle in place, swing the thread around to the top. Pull upwards to make a small, neat loop.

11 Remove the needle point, and take the thread through to the back at the top of the loop.

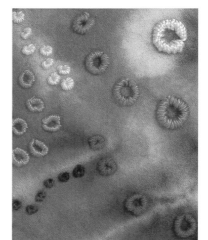

❶ *For a larger loop, use more wraps.*

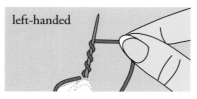

left-handed

❶ *Left-handers wrap clockwise too.*

buttonhole stitch

This stitch is often used as an edging stitch, and for working buttonholes. There are myriad variations.

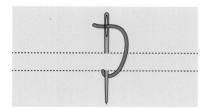

1 Use two guide lines. Bring the thread out on the lower line. To the right, insert the needle from the top to the bottom line, with the needle point over the thread.

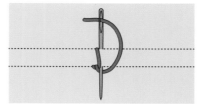

2 Pull the needle through. Insert the needle in the top line, and bring it out on the bottom line adjacent to the previous stitch.

3 Continue in the same manner. To finish stitching take a short anchoring stitch over the last buttonhole.

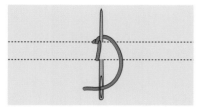

❶ *Some stitchers find it easier to have the stitching rotated 180 degrees, with the rolled section at the top rather than the bottom.*

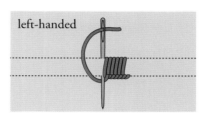

left-handed

❶ *Left-handers work this stitch in mirror image, from right to left.*

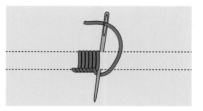

❶ *When the thread is thick, slightly angle the needle back towards the direction you have come from. This will keep the stitches looking straighter.*

slipping the end into the beginning

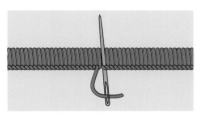

1 To join the end of the stitching up with the beginning (if working around an entire shape), slip the needle under the beginning of the first stitch.

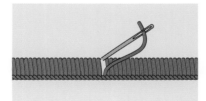

2 To finish, take the thread to the back on the top line.

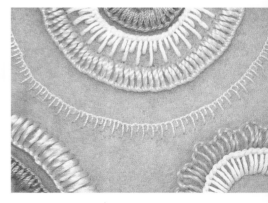

turning a sharp corner

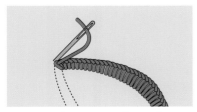

To turn a sharp corner, bring the needle out in the buttonhole at the corner point. Take a short stitch over the corner, to anchor the corner stitch.

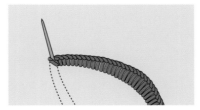

Bring the needle out again in the corner buttonhole and continue stitching in the new direction.

❶ *Taking this short anchoring stitch means that the corner stitch will sit as neatly as the rest of the stitching.*

blanket stitch

Blanket stitch, or *spaced buttonhole stitch*, is traditionally used to edge blankets, hence its name.

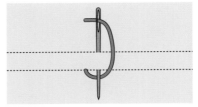

1 Use two guides. Bring the thread out on the bottom line. A little to the right, insert the needle from the top to the bottom line. Take the thread under the needle point.

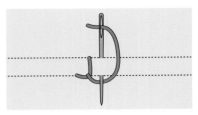

2 Pull the needle through. Moving right, and using the same spacing as before, again insert the needle from the top to the bottom line. Take the thread under the needle point.

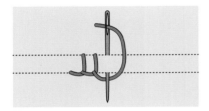

3 Pull the needle through. Moving right again, make another stitch as before.

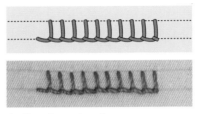

4 Continue in the same way to build up a line of blanket stitch. To finish, take a short stitch over the final stitch.

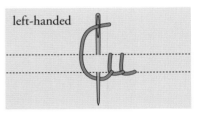

left-handed

❶ *For left-handers, the method is flipped, and worked right to left.*

closed buttonhole stitch

This is a decorative spaced buttonhole stitch.

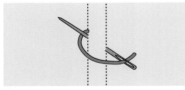

1 Use two guides. Bring the thread out on the left line. A little below, insert the needle diagonally from the right to the left line, bringing it out just below where the thread emerged. Take the thread under the needle point.

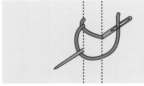

2 Pull the needle through. Diagonally insert the needle in the right line, in the same hole as the right end of the first stitch. Using the same stitch length as before, bring the needle out on the left line. Take the thread under the needle point.

3 Pull the needle through. A little below, insert the needle diagonally from the right to the left line, bringing it out just below where the thread emerged. Take the thread under the needle point.

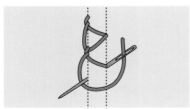

4 Using the same spacing and stitch length as earlier, diagonally insert the needle from the right to the left line. Take the thread under the needle point.

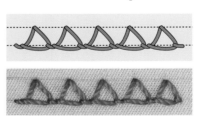

5 Continue in the same way to build up a line of stitching. To finish, take a short stitch over the final buttonhole stitch. Turn the work 90 degrees anticlockwise to get the final effect.

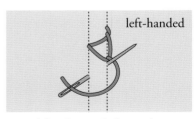

left-handed

❶ *Left-handers work this stitch in mirror image.*

crossed buttonhole stitch

This is another decorative spaced buttonhole stitch.

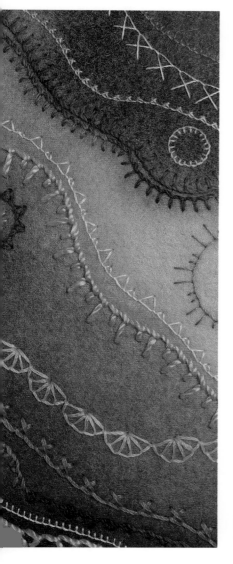

1 Use a line of squares as guides. Bring the thread out in the top left corner of the top square. Insert the needle from the bottom right to the top left of the second square. Take the thread under the needle point.

2 Pull the needle through. Insert the needle from the top right to the bottom left of the second square. Take the thread under the needle point.

3 Pull the needle through. Insert the needle from the bottom right to the top left of the fourth square. Take the thread under the needle point.

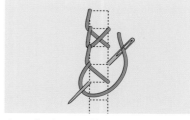

4 Pull the needle through. Insert the needle from the top right to the bottom left of the fourth square. Take the thread under the needle point.

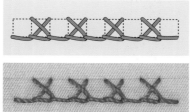

5 Continue in the same manner, to build up a line of stitching. To finish, take a stitch over the final buttonhole stitch. For the final effect, turn the work 90 degrees anticlockwise.

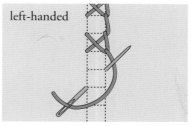

left-handed

❶ *For left-handers, the method is flipped, and worked right to left.*

knotted buttonhole stitch

This is yet another variation of blanket stitch/spaced buttonhole stitch.

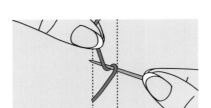

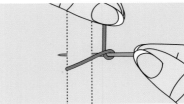

1 Using two guide lines, bring the thread out on the left line. Take the thread up over the front of the needle and around it once.

2 Without allowing the thread to slip off the point of the needle, insert the needle point in the right line, a little way up.

3 Bring the needle point out on the left line.

❶ *Do not pull the needle all the way through yet.*

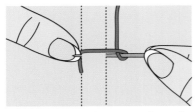

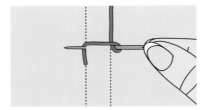

4 Lift the thread coming from the fabric up and tuck it behind the needle point.

5 Tighten the thread around the needle.

6 Pull the needle through to complete the first knotted buttonhole stitch.

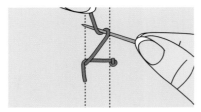

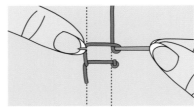

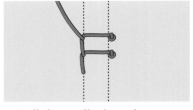

7 Take the thread up over the front of the needle and around it once.

8 Using the same spacing as before, insert the needle from the right to the left line. Tuck the thread behind the needle point, and tighten the thread around the needle.

9 Pull the needle through.

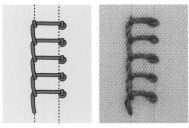

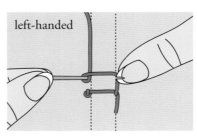

10 Continue in the same way to build up a line of stitching. To finish, take a short stitch over the final buttonhole stitch.

left-handed

❶ *Left-handers work this stitch in mirror image.*

buttonhole wheel

These can be worked with or without a gap in the centre.

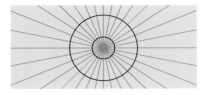

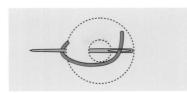

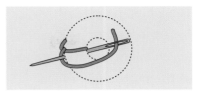

❶ *Imagine a series of lines radiating out from the centre of a circle. The needle will need to be inserted in line with the radiating guides.*

1 Bring the thread out on the outer circle. Insert the needle on the inner circle, and bring it out on the outer circle a little way around. Take the thread under the needle point.

2 Pull the needle through. Just below the previous stitch, insert the needle on the inner circle, and bring it out on the outer line, using the same spacing as previously.

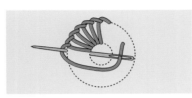

3 Continue in the same manner.
❶ *For ease of inserting the needle, turn the work around as required.*

4 For the final stitch, slip the needle under the beginning of the first stitch, towards the centre.

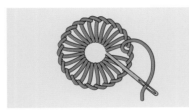

5 Insert the needle in the space at the inner circle.

6 Pull the needle through to complete the wheel.

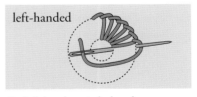

❶ *For stitches extending to the centre, less stitches are required, as it is difficult to squeeze many into the centre.*

❶ *Left-handers stitch the other way around the circle.*

buttonhole eyelet

A buttonhole wheel that deliberately creates a central hole.

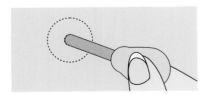

1 Make a hole in the centre of the eyelet with an awl, bodkin or stiletto. This will push the threads aside, leaving space to start the eyelet.

2 Buttonhole around the circle, inserting the needle in the centre hole for each stitch.
❶ *For a larger hole, tighten the thread after each stitch to increase tension.*

3 Complete the eyelet as for the buttonhole wheel.

whipped buttonhole stitch

The whipping creates a raised surface of extra ridges which mimic the appearance of the buttonhole rolled edge.

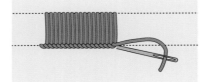

1 Work regular buttonhole using a long stitch length. Finish with a small stitch over the last buttonhole stitch.

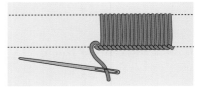

2 Change to a tapestry needle. Bring a new thread out at the beginning end of the stitching.

❶ *A tapestry needle slides easily under the stitches, without catching them.*

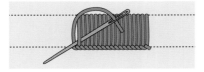

3 Slide the needle under the first stitch from the right. Ensure the thread is above the needle.

❶ *Do not enter the fabric.*

4 Gently pull the thread down towards the looped section of the buttonhole to lock the stitch in place.

5 With the thread above, slide the needle from the right, under the next buttonhole stitch. Gently pull the thread down to lock the stitch in place.

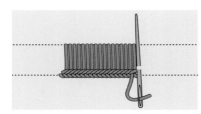

6 Continue in the same way to whip each buttonhole stitch. To finish the row, take a small stitch into the fabric, coming out just above the previous row, ready to start the next.

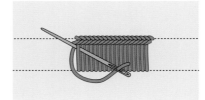

7 Turn the work 180 degrees, to facilitate ease of inserting the needle. Slide the needle under the left-most stitch from right to left. Ensure the thread is below the needle.

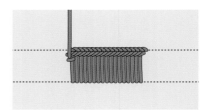

8 Gently pull the thread up towards the looped section of the buttonhole to lock the stitch in place.

9 With the thread below, slide the needle from the right, under the next buttonhole stitch. Gently pull the thread up to lock the stitch in place.

10 Continue in the same manner to complete the row.

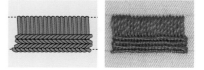

11 Work back and forth along the buttonholes stitches, turning the work as necessary, to work the desired number of whipped buttonhole rows.

❶ *When worked on a buttonhole wheel, whipping can be in one direction as shown here, or rounds can change direction as for the straight version.*

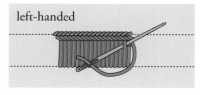

left-handed

❶ *Left-handers work this stitch in mirror image.*

tailor's buttonhole stitch

Tailor's buttonhole is worked so that a plaited edge forms where the regular rolled buttonhole edge would normally be. It is a strong and sturdy edging.

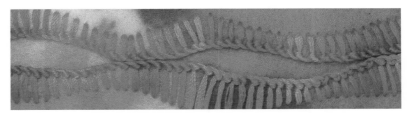

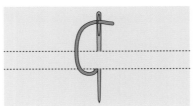

1 Use two guide lines. Bring the thread out on the bottom line. Insert the needle vertically from top to bottom, just right of the thread.

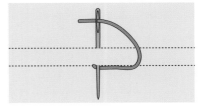

2 Take the thread under the needle point from left to right.

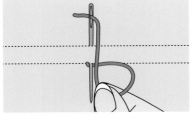

3 Take the part of the thread leading to the eye, and bring it down over the lower part of the loop.

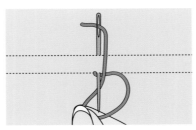

4 Still holding the same part of the thread, take it down and to the left under the needle point, making a loop around the needle point.

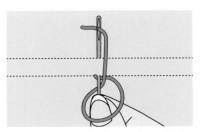

5 Pull the needle down through the loop.

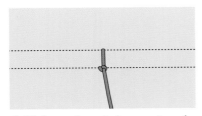

6 Tighten the stitch, creating the beginning of a plait.

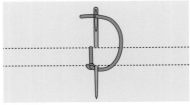

7 Insert the needle vertically from top to bottom, just right of the previous stitch, with the thread under the needle point.

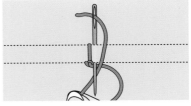

8 Take the top of the thread down and to the left under the needle point.

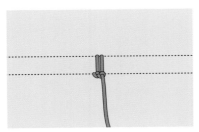

9 Pull the needle down through the loop, and tighten the stitch.

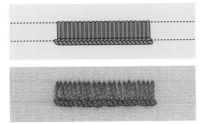

10 Continue in the same manner to build up a line of stitching.

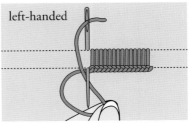

left-handed

❶ *For left-handers, the method is flipped, and worked right to left.*

up and down buttonhole stitch

This stitch has many variations. A few are shown, and you can probably devise more.

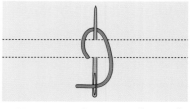

1 Use two guides. Bring the needle out on the lower one. Just right, insert it from the bottom to the top line. Take the thread under the needle point.

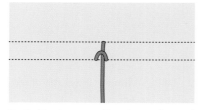

2 Pull the needle through and down.

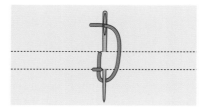

3 A little right, insert the needle from the top to the bottom line. Take the thread under the needle point.

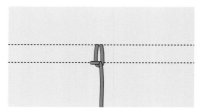

4 Pull the needle through.

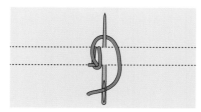

5 A little right, insert the needle from the bottom to the top line. Take the thread under the needle point.

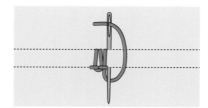

6 Pull the needle through. Insert it from the top to the bottom, with the thread under the needle point.

7 Continue to alternate up and down stitches to build up a line of stitching.
❶ *Left-handers work in the same way.*

straight variation 1

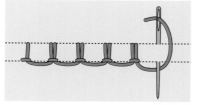

Leave a space before each 'down' stitch.

straight variation 2

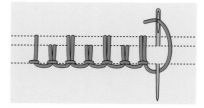

Leave space before 'down' stitches, and alternate pairs longer or shorter.

straight variation 3

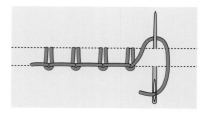

Leave a space before each 'up' stitch.

angled variation

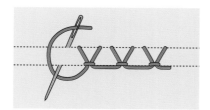

Work as for straight variation 1, but with angled stitches.

alternating variation 1

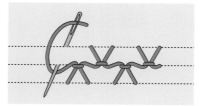

A variation on the angled variation, work alternate 'v's upside-down.

alternating variation 2

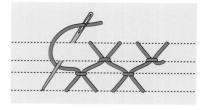

Space the alternate 'v's further apart.

open buttonhole filling stitch

Even loop tension is the most difficult aspect of this filling stitch.

1 Bring the needle out in the top left of the shape.

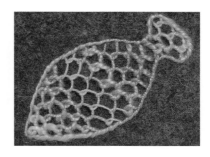

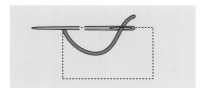

2 A little way along the top, take the needle under a few threads of fabric, from right to left. Keep the thread under the needle point.

3 Pull the needle through. Leave the thread hanging down in a gentle curve. The same distance along, take another stitch in the top line. Keep the thread under the needle point.

4 Continue in the same way to complete the row, finishing in the top right corner.

❶ *Keep the tension as even as possible.*

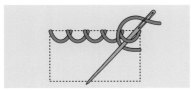

5 Bring the needle out a short way down the right side. From above, slide the needle under the right-most stitch in the top row, with the thread under the needle point.

❶ *Do not enter the fabric.*

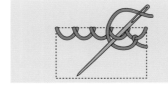

6 Pull the needle through. Leave the thread hanging down in a gentle curve. Slide the needle under the next stitch, with the thread under the needle point.

❶ *Do not enter the fabric.*

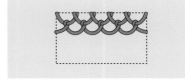

7 Continue in the same way to complete the row. Finish by taking the thread to the back on the left line.

❶ *Keep the tension as even as possible.*

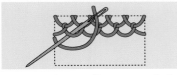

8 Bring the needle out just below. From above, slide it under the first full stitch in the previous row, with the thread under the needle point.

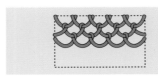

9 Keeping tension even, complete the remainder of the row.

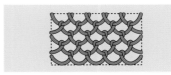

10 In a similar manner, complete the remaining rows required to fill the shape.

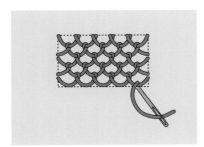

11 To hold the bottom row in place, take a short anchoring stitch over the centre bottom of each loop.

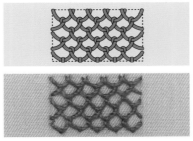

12 The completed open buttonhole filling.

left-handed

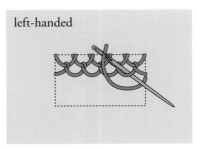

❶ *For left-handers, the method is flipped.*

buttonhole filling with return

The laid return stitch makes this a firm detached filling stitch.

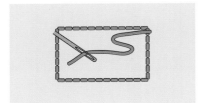

1 Outline the shape in back stitch. Level with the first stitch down each side, take a stitch from outside the right edge to outside the left edge.

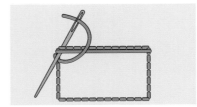

2 Bring the thread out just below the laid stitch's end. Change to a tapestry needle. Without entering the fabric, slide the needle under the first back stitch and the laid stitch, from above. Take the thread under the needle point.

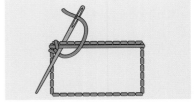

3 Pull the needle through. Take a stitch under the next back stitch and the laid stitch. Take the thread under the needle point.

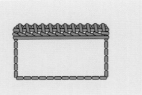

4 Work a stitch into each back stitch and the laid stitch across the row. Finish the row outside the shape, on the right edge. Lay a thread across, level with the next back stitch down the side.

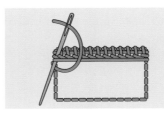

5 Bring the thread out on the left edge. Work a buttonhole into the bottom section of the last buttonhole of the previous row, and the laid thread.

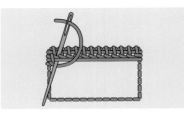

6 Work a stitch into the next buttonhole of the previous row, and the laid stitch.

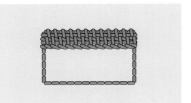

7 Continue working across the row, with a stitch into each of the previous stitches, also taking in the laid thread.
❶ *There is an extra stitch in this row, compared to the first row.*

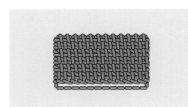

8 Continue working rows, laying threads and with each row having one more or one less stitch than the previous row.

9 For the final row, lay the thread as before. Work a buttonhole into the buttonhole stitch, the laid stitch and the first back stitch along the bottom edge of the outline.

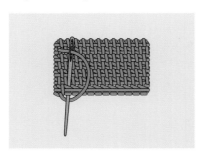

10 Stitch through the next buttonhole, the laid stitch and the next back stitch along.

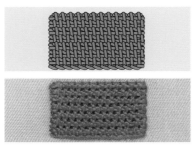

11 Continue in the same way to complete the final row. Take the thread to the back at the far edge.

left-handed

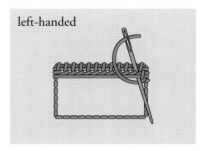

❶ *Left-handers work buttonhole filling in mirror image.*

fancy buttonhole filling

This filling is based on up and down buttonhole stitch.

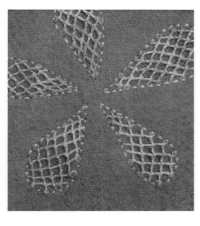

1 Outline in back stitch. Change to a tapestry needle. Bring the thread to the front outside the left side's top back stitch. From above, slide the needle under the second nearest back stitch. Take the thread under the needle point.

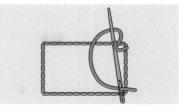

2 Pull the needle through, but leave the loop hanging down gently. From below, slide the needle under the same back stitch as before. Take the thread under the needle point.

3 Pull the needle through. From above, slide the needle under the back stitch two along. Take the thread under the needle point.

4 Pull the needle through. With the same tension as before, leave the loop hanging down gently. From below, slide the needle under the same back stitch as before. Take the thread under the needle point.

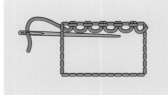

5 In the same manner, and with careful tension, fill the rest of the row. On completion, slide the needle from the left under the first back stitch at the side. Then slide the needle under the second stitch, from the right.

6 From above, slide the needle under the first loop that hangs down in the previous row. Take the thread under the needle point.

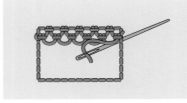

7 Keeping careful tension, continue working up and down buttonhole stitch into each of the loops that hang down. At the conclusion of the row, slide the needle under the back stitch second from the top.

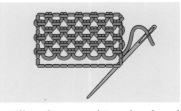

8 Fill each row, taking the thread under the back stitches at the ends of the rows. To begin the final row, slide the needle under the side back stitch and under the first back stitch in the bottom row.

9 Work the final row, sliding the needle under the bottom row of back stitch in between buttonhole stitches.

10 To finish, take the thread to the back at the outline.

left-handed

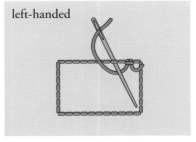

❶ *For left-handers, the method is the same, but the needle is angled from the left-hand side.*

buttonhole bars

Buttonhole bars can be worked as a surface stitch or as a stabilising element on areas of cutwork.

1 Bring the thread out at the right end of the bar's position. Take the thread to the back at the other end.

2 Bring the needle out just below the end of the first stitch. Take the thread to the back just below the right end of the first stitch.

3 Bring the needle out just below the right end of the previous stitch. Take the thread to the back just below the left end of the previous stitch.

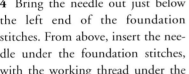

4 Bring the needle out just below the left end of the foundation stitches. From above, insert the needle under the foundation stitches, with the working thread under the needle point.
❶ *Do not enter the fabric.*

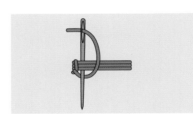

5 Pull the needle through. Work another buttonhole stitch just right of the previous one.
❶ *Do not enter the fabric.*

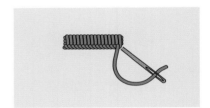

6 Continue working buttonholes to fill the bar. Take the thread to the back at the bottom of the right end of the bar.
❶ *Ensure the bar is well filled with stitches.*

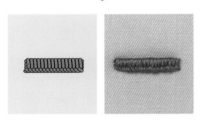

7 The completed buttonhole bar.

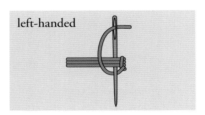

left-handed

❶ *Left-handers work this stitch in mirror image.*

buttonhole picot

Buttonhole picots are also known as *Venetian picots*.

1 Buttonhole the edge of the fabric up to the position of the picot, and insert a pin in the fabric edge there.

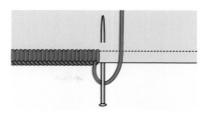

2 Loosely loop the thread from the left, under the pin head and back up over the edge of the fabric.

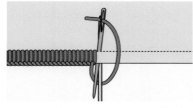

3 Using the same spacing as for the buttonholing, insert the needle in the line, bringing it out under the fabric edge, over the looped thread.

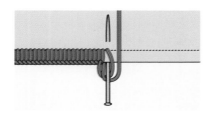

4 Pull the needle through. Leaving both threads loosely looped, take the working thread under the pin head and up over the fabric edge.

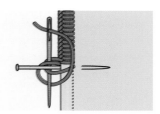

5 Turn the work 90 degrees clockwise. Slide the needle from above under the second loop's top half and the first loop's bottom half.

6 Pull the thread through to form a buttonhole stitch at the end of the loops.

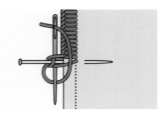

7 Slide the needle under both the picot and the pin. Take the thread behind the needle point.

8 Pull the needle through to tighten the buttonhole stitch near the end of the picot.

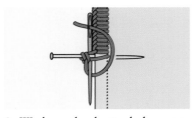

9 Work another buttonhole next to the first, under the picot and the pin.

10 Work further buttonhole stitches to fill the picot.

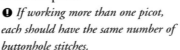
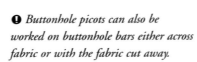

❶ *If working more than one picot, each should have the same number of buttonhole stitches.*

❶ *Buttonhole picots can also be worked on buttonhole bars either across fabric or with the fabric cut away.*

11 Turn the work 90 degrees anticlockwise back to the way it was before. Remove the pin and continue working buttonhole stitches along the edge of the fabric.

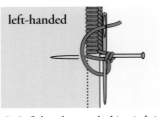

left-handed

❶ *Left-handers work this stitch in mirror image.*

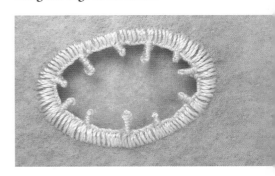

33

cable stitch

Cable stitch is a linear counted thread stitch.

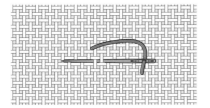

1 Use a tapestry needle, so as not to split the fabric threads. Bring the thread out of the fabric. Horizontally insert the needle two threads down and to the right, bringing it out two threads to the left.

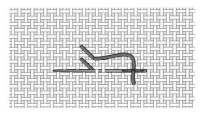

2 Pull the needle through. Vertically insert the needle two threads down and to the right. Bring it out two threads up, at the first stitch's end.

❶ *The stitches are diagonal on the fabric front. On the back, they lie parallel with the fabric threads.*

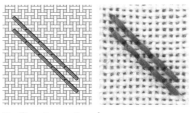

3 Pull the needle through. Horizontally insert the needle two threads down and to the right, bringing it out two threads to the left, at the end of the previous stitch.

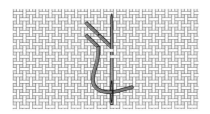

4 Pull the needle through. Vertically insert the needle two threads down and to the right. Bring it out two threads up, at the previous stitch's end.

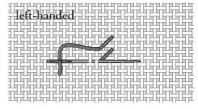

5 Continue in the same way to build up a line of cable stitch.

left-handed

❶ *Left-handers work this stitch in mirror image, travelling from the upper right to the lower left.*

turning a corner

To turn a corner, an extra stitch has to be added.

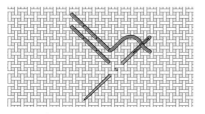

1 Work up to the stitch before the corner point. Diagonally insert the needle at the point. Bring it out two threads left and down.

❶ *This is the only time there is a diagonal stitch on the back.*

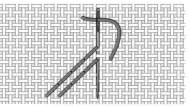

2 Pull the needle through. Turn the work 90 degrees anticlockwise. Insert the needle at the corner point again, bringing it out two threads below.

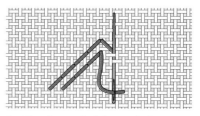

3 Continue stitching as before.

double cable stitch

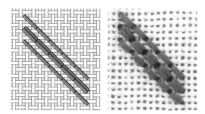

Double cable stitch has another row worked adjacent to the first.

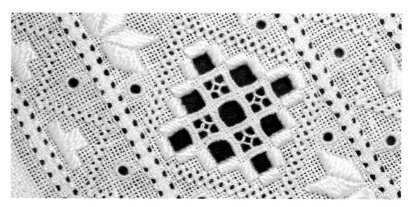

34

cable chain stitch

This pretty stitch is also known as *cable stitch*.

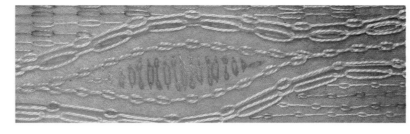

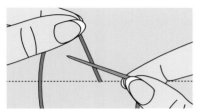

1 Use one guide. Bring the thread out on the line, and pull it upwards. Place the needle in front of the thread.

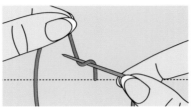

2 Wind the thread over the front of the needle and up behind it.

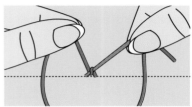

3 Insert the needle into the line a little way along from where the thread emerged.

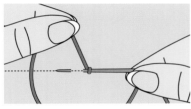

4 Bring the needle out a little further along the line (using the desired stitch length).

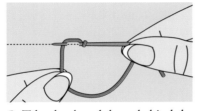

5 Take the thread down behind the needle point.
❶ *Make sure the thread sits snugly around the needle.*

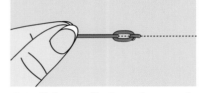

6 Pull the needle through to gently tighten the chain and link.

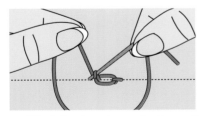

7 Wind the thread over the front of the needle and up behind it. Insert the needle into the line using the same distance as before.

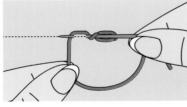

8 Bring the needle out on the line using the same stitch length as before. With the thread snug around the needle, take the thread down behind the needle point.

9 Continue in the same manner, to build up a line of stitches. To finish, take a short stitch over the end of the last chain.

starting a new thread

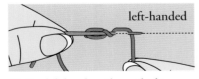

❶ *For left-handers, the method is flipped, and worked left to right.*

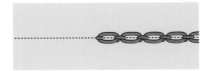

1 Finish the thread with a small stitch over the last chain. Fasten the thread in the back of the stitching.

2 Fasten the new thread at the back. Bring it out in the last chain. Continue stitching as before.

stepped cable chain stitch

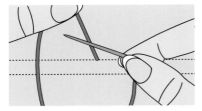

1 Use two guides. Bring the thread out on the top line, and pull it upwards. Place the needle in front of the thread.

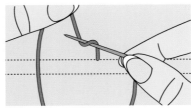

2 Wind the thread over the front of the needle and up behind it.

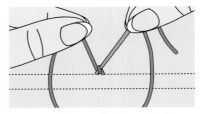

3 Insert the needle into the line a little way along from where the thread emerged.

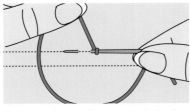

4 Bring the needle out a little further along the line (using the desired stitch length).

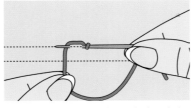

5 Take the thread down behind the needle point.
❶ *Make sure the thread sits snugly around the needle.*

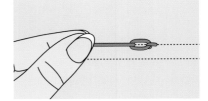

6 Pull the needle through to gently tighten the chain and link.

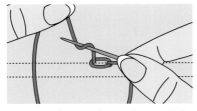

7 With the needle in front of the thread, wind the thread over the front of the needle and up behind it.

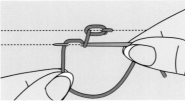

8 Insert the needle into the lower line, and bring it out again using the same stitch length as before. When the thread is snug around the needle, take the thread down behind the needle point.

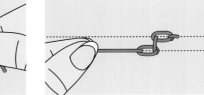

9 Pull the needle through to gently tighten the chain and link.

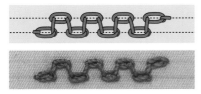

10 Work subsequent chains on alternate lines to build up a row of stitches. To finish, take a short stitch over the end of the last chain.

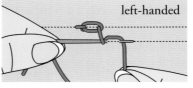

left-handed

❶ *For left-handers, the method is flipped, and worked left to right.*

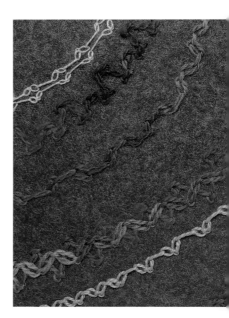

zigzagging cable chain stitch

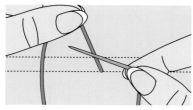

1 Use two guide lines. Bring the thread out on the lower line, and pull it upwards. Place the needle in front of the thread.

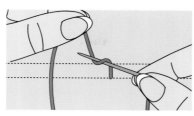

2 Wind the thread over the front of the needle and up behind it.

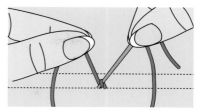

3 Insert the needle into the lower line a little way along from where the thread emerged.

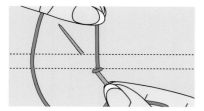

4 Angle the needle, and bring it out on the top line.

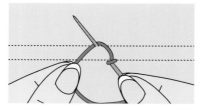

5 Take the thread behind the needle point from right to left.
❶ *Make sure the thread sits snugly around the needle.*

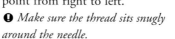

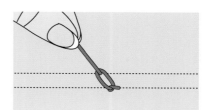

6 Pull the needle through to complete the first chain.

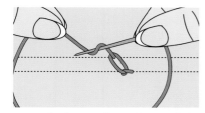

7 With the needle in front of the thread, wind the thread over the front of the needle and up behind it.

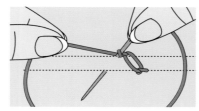

8 Insert the needle in the top line, and using the opposite angle to before, bring the needle out on the lower line.

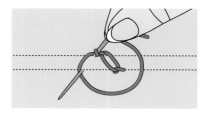

9 Take the thread behind the needle point from left to right.
❶ *Make sure the thread sits snugly around the needle.*

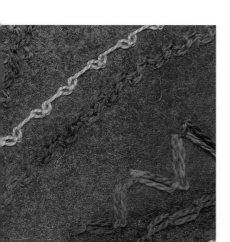

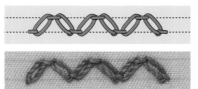

10 Pull the needle through to complete the next chain.
❶ *Note the link between the chains.*

12 Continue cycling through the steps to build up a line of zigzagging cable chain. To finish, anchor the last chain with a short stitch.

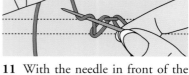

11 With the needle in front of the thread, wind the thread over the front of the needle and up behind it.

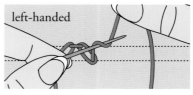

left-handed

❶ *For left-handers, the method is flipped, and worked left to right.*

cable plait stitch
This stitch is also known as *braid stitch* or *figure of eight*.

1 Use two guides, about 2 mm (¹/₁₂ in) apart. Bring the thread out on the left line. Lay it over the needle.
❶ *If it is too wide it becomes unstable.*

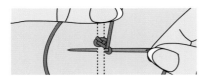

4 Just below where the thread emerges from the left line, insert the needle in the right line and bring it out on the left line.

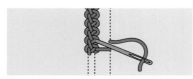

7 Moving down a little, work the next stitch below the previous one.
❶ *Too close, and it all looks crammed.*

starting a new thread

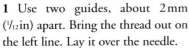

To finish, take a short stitch over the last stitch. Fasten the old and new threads on the back. Bring the needle out in lowest left loop of the stitching. Continue as before.

2 Pull the needle through. Bring the needle out on the line level with the next plait and make a stitch into it.

2 Take the thread up behind the needle point.

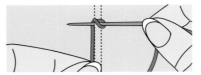

5 Take the thread down behind the needle point. Gently tighten so the knot fits snugly around the needle.
❶ *If you do not tighten the stitch at this point, the plait will not be neat.*

8 Continue, in the same manner. To finish, take a short stitch over the bottom of the final plait.

overcast cable plait stitch

Overcasting helps to anchor the stitching in place, which can be useful if the cable plait stitch needs to be wide. It also gives a very different look to the cable plaits.

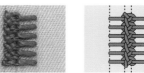

3 Continue in the same way until all the stitches have been overcast.
❶ *The length of the overcast stitch can be short, long or variable.*

3 Hold the thread above the needle, and move the needle up and right, making sure the loop remains on the needle.

6 Pull the needle through to gently tighten the stitch.
❶ *When tightening, pull to the left only, as this will allow the stitch to tighten whilst maintaining its shape.*

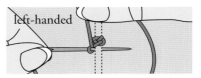

left-handed

❶ *For left-handers, the method is worked in mirror image, with the needle going in from left to right.*

1 Work a line of cable plait stitch. Bring the needle out on a new guide next to the stitching, level with the first plait. Insert the needle into the loop on the right side of the plait.

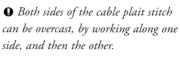

❶ *Both sides of the cable plait stitch can be overcast, by working along one side, and then the other.*

cast on stitch

This stitch is most often used in Brazilian embroidery. Use a milliner's or straw needle.

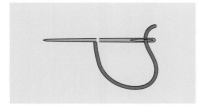

1 Bring the needle out of the fabric. Take a short stitch, coming out where the thread emerged previously. ❶ *Do not pull the needle through yet.*

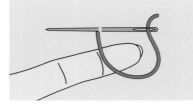

2 Place your left forefinger in the loop, from behind.

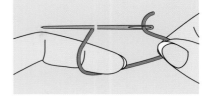

3 Hold the thread near the needle with your right hand to tension the thread. Begin turning the top of your left finger towards you.

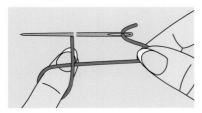

4 Keep turning until your finger is nail up.

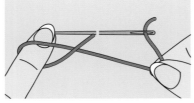

5 Move your finger up towards the needle tip.

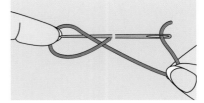

6 Gently place your finger on the needle tip.

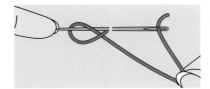

7 With your right hand pull the thread so that the loop slips off your finger and onto the needle.

8 Pull the thread downwards so that it sits snug around the needle at the point where the needle comes out of the fabric.

9 Create another loop in the same way as before.

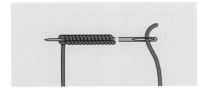

10 Work more loops as necessary.

11 With your right hand, hold the loops loosely on the needle. Gently pull the needle through with your left hand.

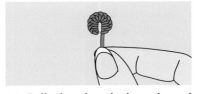

12 Pull the thread through and tighten it into a rounded loop.

13 Insert the needle at the base of the right side of the loop.

14 The completed cast on stitch.

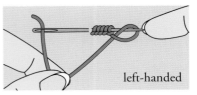

❶ *For left-handers, the method is flipped, and worked left to right.*

double cast on stitch

Master regular cast on stitch first, then use those skills to apply to this double version. This stitch is often used in Brazilian embroidery. Use a milliner's needle.

1 Thread the needle and bring the ends together to make a doubled thread. Bring the doubled thread out of the fabric.

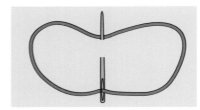

2 Take a stitch from below, bringing the needle out again where the threads emerged.

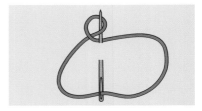

3 Take the left part of the thread in hand, twist it into a loop as shown and slip it onto the needle point.

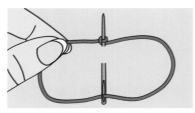

4 Tighten the thread around the needle.

5 Take the right part of the thread in hand, twist it into a loop and slip it onto the needle point.

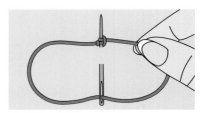

6 Tighten the thread around the needle.

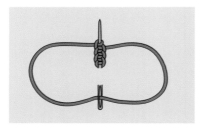

7 Twist a left loop and slip it onto the needle, then a right loop. Continue in the same manner until there are enough stitches on the needle to span the distance to where the needle is inserted in the fabric.

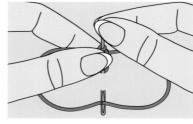

8 Gently hold the stitches to keep them steady, and pull the needle through with your right hand.

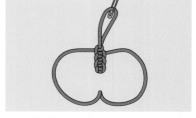

9 Pull the needle up and bring the two threads all the way through the cast on stitches.

10 Take the needle to the back at the bottom, where the needle previously entered the fabric, and pull the stitch down against the fabric.

11 The completed double cast on stitch.

❶ *Left-handers work this stitch in the same way.*

40

ceylon stitch

This stitch looks like knitting when worked close together. When spaced further apart, it looks like columns of plaits. It is similar to vandyke stitch, which has a single plaited column.

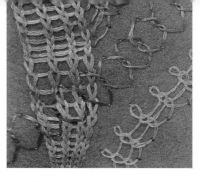

1 Bring the needle out at the top of the shape, near the right edge. Insert the needle just below. Bring the needle out again further along the top edge.
❶ *The stitch spacing determines the spacing between the plaits.*

2 Make a short stitch as before, bringing the needle out again the same distance away as previously, on the top line.

3 Work evenly spaced short stitches across the top of the shape.

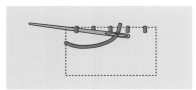

4 Change to a tapestry needle. Bring the needle out on the shape's left side, a short way below. Slide the needle from right to left under the closest stitch.
❶ *Use loose tension and do not enter the fabric.*

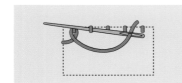

5 Leaving the stitch hanging down loosely, slide the needle from right to left under the next stitch.
❶ *Keep the tension even across the row.*

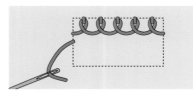

6 Continue working in the same way, to fill the width. Take the thread to the back on the right side. Bring the needle out again short way down on the left side.

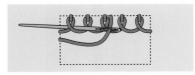

7 Slide the needle from right to left under the closest crossed stitches.
❶ *Continue with the same tension as for the previous row.*

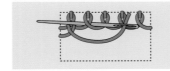

8 Leaving the stitch hanging down loosely, slide the needle from right to left under the next crossed stitches.

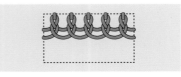

9 Continue across, to fill the row. Take the thread to the back on the right side.

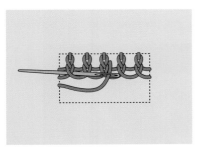

10 Work across the next row in the same way as for previous rows.

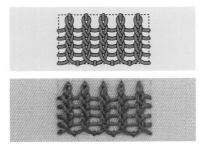

11 Continue with rows of looping stitches to fill the shape. To finish, take a small stitch over the bottom of each loop to hold them in place.

left-handed

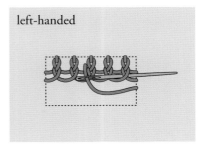

❶ *For left-handers, the method is flipped, and worked from the right to the left.*

ladder stitch

This variation of Ceylon stitch forms a ladder with a single plait down each side, right at the edge.

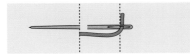

1 Use two guides. Bring the needle out on the left line. Slightly above and to the right of where the thread emerges, take a short stitch, exiting on the left line.

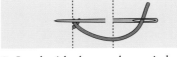

2 Level with that, make a stitch of the same length, inserting the needle in the right line.

❶ *Leave the thread between the two stitches hanging loosely between the lines.*

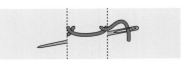

3 Insert the needle in the right line, level with where the thread emerged in the left line at the very beginning. Bring the needle out on the left line a short way below.

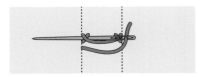

4 Slide the needle from right to left under the crossed stitches on the left.

❶ *It can be difficult to get the plaits to stay left at the edges of the stitches. To assist, give the thread a gentle tug to pull it to the left.*

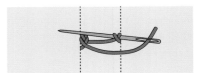

5 Slide the needle from right to left under the crossed stitches on the right.

❶ *Leave the thread between the two stitches hanging loosely between the lines.*

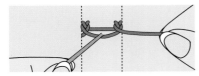

❶ *Temporarily insert a needle above the middle loop so that it can't be pulled up tight. Gently tug the thread to the right to ensure the plait stays on the right edge.*

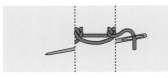

6 Insert the needle in the right line, level with where it emerged on the left line. Bring it out on the left line using the same spacing as before.

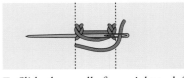

7 Slide the needle from right to left under the lowest crossed stitches on the left.

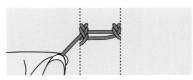

❶ *Give the thread a gentle tug to pull the plait to the left.*

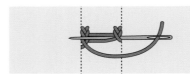

8 Slide the needle from right to left under the lowest crossed stitches on the right edge.

❶ *Leave the thread between the two stitches hanging loosely between the lines.*

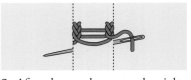

9 After the gentle tug to the right, insert the needle in the right line, level with where it emerged on the left line. Bring it out on the left line using the same spacing as before.

10 Continue stitching in the same way. To finish, take the needle and thread to the back on the right line. Anchor the lowest 'ladder rung' with a short stitch near each plait.

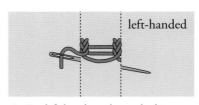

left-handed

❶ *For left-handers, the method is worked in mirror image, with the needle inserted from left to right.*

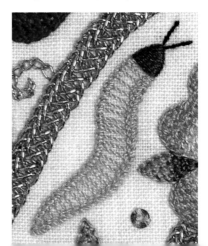

42

chain stitch

Chain stitch is usually a linear stitch, but can also be used as a filling or for padding under other stitches. There are many variations of chain stitch. Also known as *tambour stitch* and *point de chainette*.

1 Use one guide line. Bring the thread out on the line. From the right, insert the needle at the same point and bring it out again further along the line. Loop the thread underneath the needle point.

2 Pull the needle through. From the right, insert the needle into the first chain, on the line where the thread emerges. Bring the needle point back out again further along the line and take the thread under it.

3 Repeat to build up a line of chain stitches. To finish, anchor the final chain by taking a short stitch over its end.

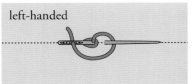
left-handed

❶ *For left-handers, the method is flipped, and worked right to left.*

starting a new thread

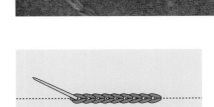

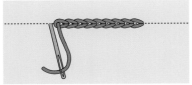 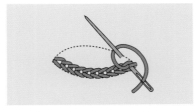

1 To finish a thread, take a short stitch over the last chain. Fasten the thread at the back of the stitching.

2 Fasten the new thread. Bring the needle out in the last chain. Continue stitching.

turning a sharp corner

1 To turn a sharp corner without a break in the stitching, work up to the corner and take a short stitch over the end to finish off. Bring the needle out in the last chain.

2 Insert the needle in the chain, and bring the needle out again, a stitch length along. Loop the thread under the needle point.

3 Pull the needle through, and continue stitching.

twisted chain stitch

A simple chain variation, which can be used in a line or singly.

1 Use one guide. Bring the thread out on the line. Insert the needle just below where the thread emerges. Bring it out on the line a little further along to the left. Take the thread down across the needle and then up behind the needle point.

2 Pull the needle through to gently tighten the twisted chain.

3 Using the same needle angle and stitch length as before, insert the needle outside the previous chain, just below where the thread emerges. Bring the needle out on the line. Take the thread down across the needle and up behind the needle point.

left-handed

4 Continue in the same manner. To finish, take a short stitch over the last chain.

❶ *Left-handers work this stitch from left to right.*

❶ *Twisted chains can also be worked singly, and scattered in a pattern or randomly, to create a powdered filling.*

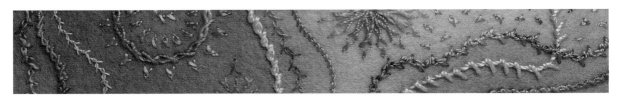

alternating twisted chain stitch

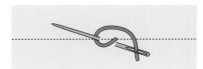  

1 Bring the thread out on the line. Insert the needle just below where the thread emerges. Bring it out on the line a little further along to the left. Take the thread down across the needle and then up behind the needle point.

2 Pull the needle through to gently tighten the twisted chain.

3 Using the same stitch length as before, insert the needle outside the previous chain, above where the thread emerges. Bring the needle out on the line. Take the thread up across the needle then down behind the needle point.

  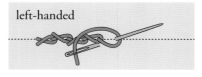

left-handed

4 Pull the needle through. Insert the needle just below where the thread emerges. Bring it out on the line. Take the thread down across the needle and up behind the needle point.

5 Continue in the same manner, alternating from side to side for each subsequent stitch. To finish, take a short stitch over the last chain.

❶ *Left-handers work this stitch from left to right.*

zigzagging chain stitch

Zigzagging chain stitch is also known as *vandyke chain stitch*.

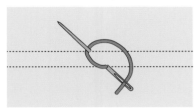

1 Use two guide lines. Bring the needle out on the bottom line. Diagonally insert the needle in the same hole as where the thread emerged, bringing it out on the top line. Take the thread under the needle point from left to right.

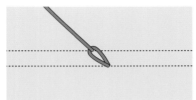

2 Pull the needle through.

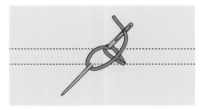

3 Diagonally insert the needle into the chain, in the top line. Using the same stitch length as before, bring the needle out on the bottom line. Take the thread under the needle point from left to right.

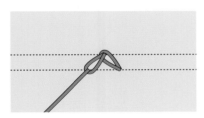

4 Pull the needle through.

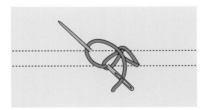

5 Diagonally insert the needle into the previous chain in the bottom line, and using the same stitch length as before, bring the needle out on the top line. Take the thread under the needle point from left to right.

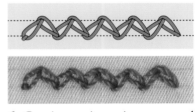

6 Continue zigzagging up and down to build up a line of stitching. To finish, take a short stitch over the last chain.

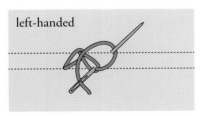

left-handed

❶ *Left-handers work this stitch in mirror image, from left to right.*

detached chain stitch

Detached chain stitches are single chains and can be used alone, in groups as flowers, or worked side by side as a filler. Also known as *daisy stitch*, *lazy daisy stitch*, *loop stitch*, *picot stitch*, *tail chain stitch* and *tied loop stitch*.

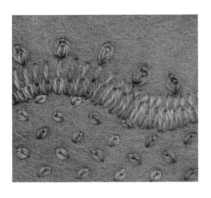

1 Bring the thread out of the fabric. Insert the needle into the same hole and bring it out a short distance away. Take the thread under the needle point.

2 Gently pull the needle through. Take a short stitch over the end to finish.

❶ *Don't pull so tight that the sides of the chain go straight. They should gently curve.*

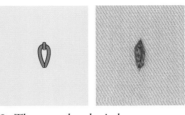

3 The completed stitch.

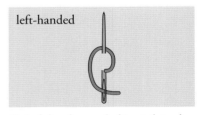

left-handed

❶ *Left-handers work this stitch in the same way.*

side by side

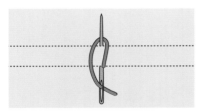

1 Use two guide lines. Bring the thread out on the bottom line. Insert the needle immediately to the left of where the thread emerges. Bring the needle out on the top line. Take the thread behind the needle point from right to left.

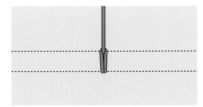

2 Pull the needle through to tighten the chain so that the sides almost lie straight.

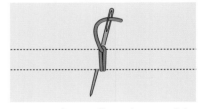

3 Insert the needle at the top of the chain, bringing it out on the bottom line, just left of the previous stitch.

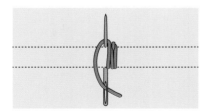

4 Pull the needle through. Insert the needle immediately to the left of where the thread emerges. Bring the needle out on the top line. Take the thread behind the needle point from right to left.

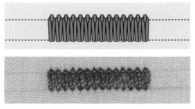

5 Continue working chain stitches next to each other to fill the area required.

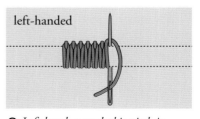

left-handed

❶ *Left-handers work this stitch in mirror image, from left to right.*

46

lazy daisy

1 To work a five-petalled flower, work the first chain stitch petal angled towards 12 o'clock.

2 Work the next petal angled towards 5 o'clock.

3 Work the third petal angled towards 7 o'clock.

❶ *Turn the fabric if it helps with inserting the needle comfortably.*

4 Work the fourth petal angled towards 10 o'clock.

5 Work the fifth petal angled towards 2 o'clock.

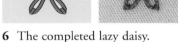

6 The completed lazy daisy.

inside-out lazy daisy

1 From 12 o'clock to the centre of the clock, work a short chain stitch, with a long anchoring stitch that ends up in the centre of the flower.

2 Work the next petal in the same way from 5 o'clock to the centre.

❶ *Turn the fabric if it helps with inserting the needle comfortably.*

3 Work subsequent petals from 7 o'clock, 10 o'clock and 2 o'clock to the centre of the flower.

many-petalled lazy daisy

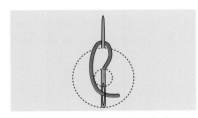

1 Use two concentric circles as guides. Work a chain stitch petal from the inner circle to the outer one.

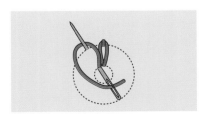

2 Moving around the circle a little way, work another petal from the inside circle to the outside one.

❶ *It may be helpful to mark the evenly spaced positions of the petals on the outer circle before working subsequent chains.*

3 Using even spacing, work around the circles to complete the flower.

❶ *Turn the work as needed to help with inserting the needle comfortably.*

whipped chain stitch

Whipped chain is worked on a foundation of regular chain stitch. The same or a contrasting coloured thread can be used. Work with a tapestry needle.

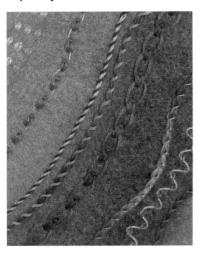

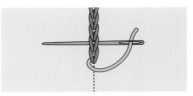

1 Work a foundation of chain stitches. Bring the thread out just under the left side of the lowest chain. Slide the needle under the next chain from the right.

❶ *Do not enter the fabric at any stage of the whipping.*

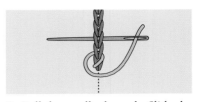

2 Pull the needle through. Slide the needle under the next chain from right to left.

3 Continue in the same manner. To finish, take the thread to the back under the right side of the last chain.

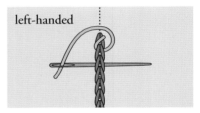

left-handed

❶ *Left-handed people work this stitch rotated 180 degrees.*

threaded chain stitch

Threaded chain is worked on a foundation row of single detached chain stitches. The same or contrasting coloured threads can be used. Work with a tapestry needle.

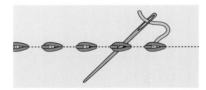

1 Work a foundation row of spaced, single, detached chain stitches. Bring the needle out from under the top of the first chain stitch from the right end. Slide the needle under the second chain from top to bottom.

❶ *Do not enter the fabric at any stage during the threading.*

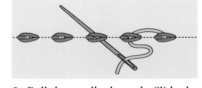

2 Pull the needle through. Slide the needle under the next chain, from bottom to top.

❶ *Leave the thread curving gently between the stitches. Do not pull it too tight.*

3 Continue threading from side to side under the chain stitches. Finish by taking the thread to the back under the final chain stitch.

❶ *If this is your desired effect, you can stop here, and not thread the other side also.*

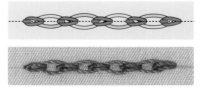

4 Starting at the beginning of the line, with a new thread, work another line of threading to fill in the gaps.

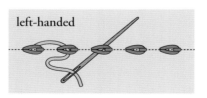

left-handed

❶ *Left-handed people work this in mirror image, from left to right.*

interlaced chain stitch

Interlaced chain is worked on a foundation of regular or square chain stitch, which has been stitched from right to left. The same or a contrasting coloured thread can be used. Work with a tapestry needle.

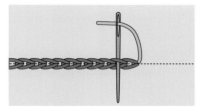

1 Bring the thread out at the right end of the chain stitch foundation. Working with the top section of each chain stitch only, slide the needle from above, under the second chain.
❶ *Do not enter the fabric at any stage.*

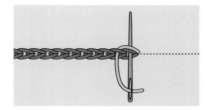

2 Pull the needle through. Slide the needle under the top parts of both the first chain and interlaced stitch, from below.
❶ *Do not pull tight. Leave the thread curving gently around the chain stitch.*

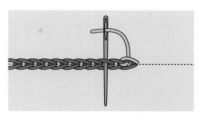

3 Pull the needle through. Slide the needle under the top section of the third chain, from above.

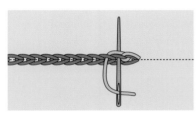

4 Pull the needle through. Slide the needle under the top part of the second chain and the second interlaced stitch, from below.

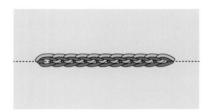

5 Continue in the same manner, interlacing each chain stitch. To finish, take the thread to the back at the end of the chain stitching.

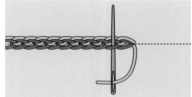

6 Bring a new thread out at the right end again. Working with the bottom section of each chain stitch only, slide the needle from below under the second chain.

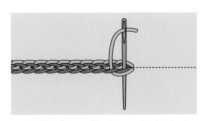

7 Pull the needle through. Slide the needle under the bottom part of the first chain and the first interlaced stitch, from above.

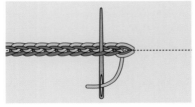

8 Pull the needle through. Slide the needle under the bottom section of the third chain, from below.

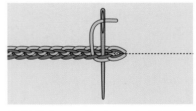

9 Pull the needle through. Slide the needle under the bottom part of the second chain and the second interlaced stitch, from above.

10 Continue in the same way to complete the line of stitching. To finish, take the thread to the back at the end of the chain stitching.

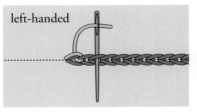

left-handed

❶ *Left-handers work this stitch in mirror image, from left to right.*

square chain stitch

1 Use two guide lines. Bring the thread out on the left line. Level with it, insert the needle in the right line. Bring the needle out on the left line a little way down. Take the thread under the needle point.

2 Pull the needle through, but leave the stitch hanging loosely.
❶ *This will allow you to comfortably insert the needle into the right side of the stitch.*

3 Level with the emerging thread, insert the needle into the chain, on the right line. Use the previous stitch length, and bring the needle out on the left line. Take the thread under the needle point. Gently tighten the previous stitch around the needle.

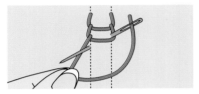

4 Pull the needle through, leaving the stitch loose. Level with the emerging thread, insert the needle into the chain, on the right line. Bring it out lower down on the left line. Take the thread under the needle point. Tighten the previous stitch around the needle.

5 Continue in the same manner to build up a line of stitching. To finish take two short stitches over the bottom chain, one on the left line, and one on the right.

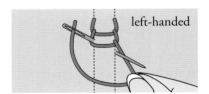

left-handed

❶ *Left-handers work in mirror image, inserting the needle from left to right.*

double chain stitch

This stitch is very similar to closed feather stitch. Here though, the stitches link into the previous chains. Double chain stitch is also known as *Turkmen stitch.*

1 Use two guides. Bring the thread out on the right line. Take a stitch down the left line, so that its middle aligns with the emerging thread. Take the thread under the needle point.

2 Pull the needle through. With the same stitch length as before, take a stitch down the right line, inserting the needle where the thread first emerged. Take the thread under the needle point.

3 Pull the needle through. With the same stitch length as before, take a stitch down the left line, inserting the needle in the bottom of the earlier chain. Take the thread under the needle point.

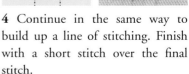

4 Continue in the same way to build up a line of stitching. Finish with a short stitch over the final stitch.
❶ *Left-handers work this stitch in exactly the same way.*

rosette chain stitch

This stitch is used for borders, and straight and curved lines.

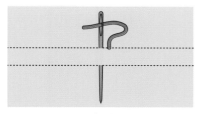

1 Use two guide lines. Bring the thread out on the top line. A little to the left, insert the needle vertically, bringing it out on the bottom line.

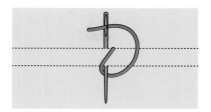

2 Take the thread to the left across the needle, and to the right behind the needle point.

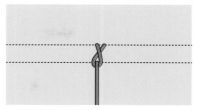

3 Pull the needle through.
❶ *This creates a slightly slanting twisted chain.*

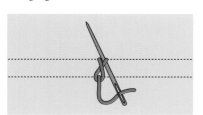

4 From below, slide the needle under the right 'arm' of the twisted chain.
❶ *Do not enter the fabric.*

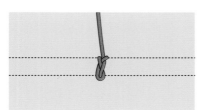

5 Pull the needle through.
❶ *Do not tighten too much or the stitch will become misshapen.*

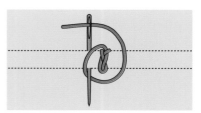

6 A little to the left, take a stitch from the top line to the bottom line. Take the thread around the needle point to make another twisted chain.

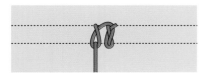

7 Pull the needle through.

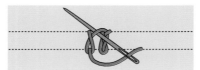

8 From below, slide the needle under the thread between the rosettes.

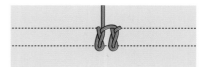

9 Pull the needle through.

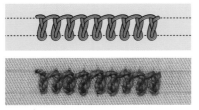

10 Continue in the same way to build up a line of stitching.

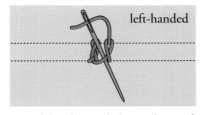

left-handed

❶ *Left-handers work this stitch turned 180 degrees.*

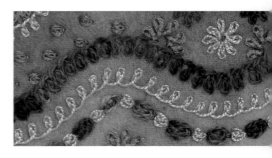

oyster stitch

This is a combination of a rosette chain and a chain stitch.

1 Work a rosette chain stitch.

2 Insert the needle right of where the thread first emerged. Bring it out at the bottom of the rosette. Take the thread under the needle point.

3 Pull the needle through. To finish, take the thread to the back over the end of the chain.

knotted chain stitch

This stitch creates very rounded chains with links in between. It is not a very stable stitch.

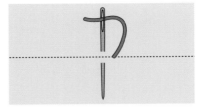

1 Use one guide line. Bring the thread out on the line. A little to the left, take a vertical stitch from just above the line to just below the line.

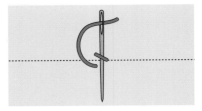

2 Pull the needle through. From above, slide the needle under the stitch.
❶ *Do not enter the fabric.*

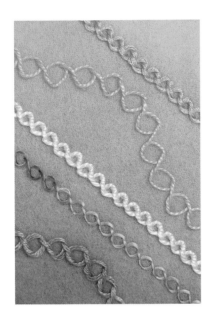

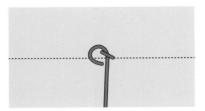

3 Pull the needle through, and leave the thread looped gently around.

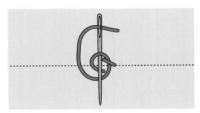

4 Slide the needle under the top and over the bottom part of the loop and the working thread.
❶ *Do not enter the fabric.*

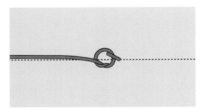
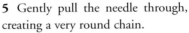

5 Gently pull the needle through, creating a very round chain.
❶ *Do not pull too tight, as this will cause misshapen chains.*

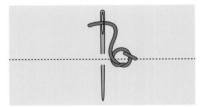

6 Using the same spacing as before, a little to the left, take a vertical stitch from just above the line to just below the line.

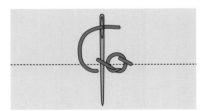
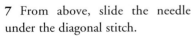

7 From above, slide the needle under the diagonal stitch.
❶ *Do not enter the fabric.*

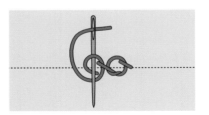

8 Pull the needle through, and leave the thread looped gently around. Slide the needle under the top, and over the bottom part of the loop, and the working thread.
❶ *Do not enter the fabric.*

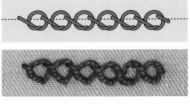

9 Continue in the same manner to build up a line of stitching.
❶ *Left-handers work this stitch in the same way as right-handers.*

magic chain stitch

Also known as *chequered chain stitch*, or *alternating chain stitch*, this is a fun stitch which rarely fails to surprise and please.

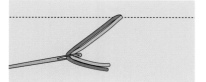

1 Use one guide line. Thread two threads, each a different colour, into a needle that is large enough to take both threads comfortably. Bring the threads out on the line.

2 Insert the needle in the line in the same hole from which the threads emerge. Bring the needle out a little way along the line. Loop one of the threads under the needle point.
❶ *Keep the other thread out of the way.*

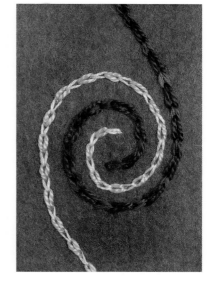

3 Pull the needle through to create a chain.
❶ *You will have to pull the unused thread a little more, so that it disappears back into the fabric.*

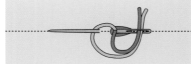

4 Insert the needle into the chain, in the same hole through which the threads emerge. Bring the needle out a little way along the line. Loop the previously unused thread under the needle point.
❶ *Keep the other thread out of the way.*

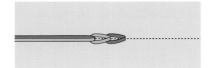

5 Pull the needle through to create the next chain.
❶ *You will have to pull the unused thread a little more, so that it disappears back into the fabric.*

6 Insert the needle into the chain, in the same hole through which the threads emerge. Bring the needle out a little way along the line. Loop the first thread under the needle point.
❶ *Keep the other thread out of the way.*

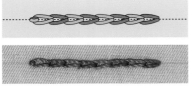

7 Continue working chain stitches, alternating the thread colours. To finish, take a short stitch over the last chain.

left-handed

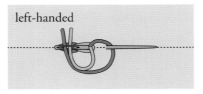

❶ *Left-handers work this stitch in mirror image, from left to right.*

reverse chain stitch

This stitch is worked in reverse compared to regular chain stitch. The 'final' stitch is worked first and subsequent stitches are worked in behind it. Stitch placement can be more precise as the needle position is more easily seen. It is useful for working with threads that are less easy to manipulate, such as metallic thread. Also known as *broad chain stitch*.

1 Use one line. Work a single chain stitch on the line, with the anchoring stitch at the top.

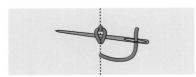

2 Bring the thread out on the line a stitch length below the first chain. Without entering the fabric, slide the needle under the chain.

3 Insert the needle where the thread emerged. Take the needle and thread through to the back.
❶ *Do not pull too tight.*

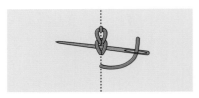

4 Bring the thread out a stitch length below. Slide the needle under the previous chain.

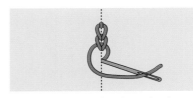

5 Insert the needle where the thread emerged. Take the needle and thread through to the back.

6 Continue in the same manner, to build up a line of stitching.

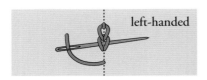
left-handed

❶ *Left-handers work this stitch in mirror image.*

heavy chain stitch

Worked similarly to reverse chain, this makes a heavier chain.

1 Use one line. Work a single chain stitch on the line, with the anchoring stitch at the top.

2 Bring the thread out on the line a stitch length below the first chain. Without entering the fabric, slide the needle under the chain's anchor stitch.

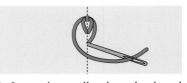

3 Insert the needle where the thread emerged. Take the needle and thread through to the back.

4 Bring the thread out on the line a stitch length below the previous chain. Slide the needle under both of the first two chains.

5 Insert the needle where the thread emerged. Take the needle and thread through to the back.

6 Bring the thread out on the line a stitch length below the previous chain. Slide the needle under the previous two chains.

 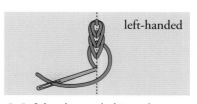

7 Insert the needle where the thread emerged. Take the needle and thread through to the back.

8 Continue in the same manner, to build up a line of stitching.

❶ *Left-handers work this stitch in mirror image.*

hungarian braided chain stitch

This variation of heavy chain, has a braided effect, making it even more decorative.

1 Use one line. Work a single chain stitch on the line, with the anchoring stitch at the top.

2 Bring the thread out on the line a stitch length below the first chain. Without entering the fabric, slide the needle under the chain's anchor stitch.

3 Take the thread to the back where it previously emerged from the fabric.

4 Bring the thread out on the line a stitch length below the previous chain. Slide the needle under the inner chain only.

5 Take the thread to the back where it previously emerged from the fabric.

6 Bring the thread out on the line a stitch length below the previous chain. Slide the needle under only the bottom section of the second last chain.

 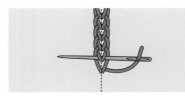 

7 Take the thread to the back where it previously emerged from the fabric.

8 Continue to build up a line of stitching. To finish, bring the thread out from under the right side near the bottom of the final chain. Slide the needle under only the bottom section of the second last chain.

9 Take the thread to the back just under the left side, near the bottom of the chain.

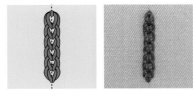 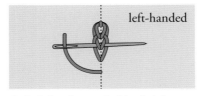

10 The completed stitch.

❶ *Left-handers work this stitch in mirror image.*

raised chain band

Raised chain band creates a very attractive braid looking stitch. The best effect is obtained with medium to thick threads. Contrasting or the same coloured threads can be used.

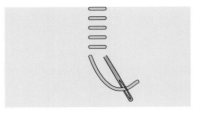

1 Work a series of short, spaced parallel stitches.

2 Change to a tapestry needle. Bring a new thread out above the middle of the top stitch. From below, slide the needle under the left half of the stitch.

3 From above, slide the needle under the right half of the top stitch. Take the thread under the needle point.

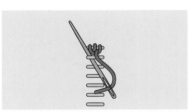

4 Pull the needle through. From below, slide the needle under the left half of the second straight stitch.

5 From above, slide the needle under the right half of the second straight stitch. Take the thread under the needle point.

6 Continue in the same way to fill all the straight stitches. To finish, take a short stitch over the final chain.

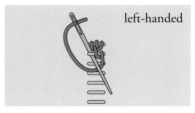

left-handed

❶ *Left-handers work this stitch in mirror image.*

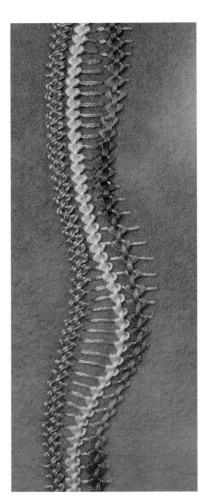

feathered chain stitch

This stitch is a cross between chain and feather stitch, and is often called *chained feather stitch*.

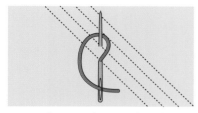

1 Use four evenly spaced guides, on a 45 degree angle. Bring the thread out on the bottom line. Insert the needle in the same hole, and bring it out directly above, on the second line. Take the thread under the needle point.

2 Pull the needle through. Take the needle to the back directly above, on the third line.

3 Bring the thread out on the top line, level with the top of the previous stitch. Insert the needle in the same hole, and bring it out, on the third line at the top of the previous stitch. Take the thread under the needle point.

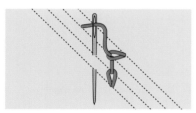

4 Pull the needle through. Insert the needle in the second line, level with where the thread emerged. Bring it out directly below, on the bottom line.

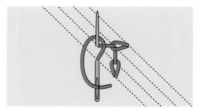

5 Pull the needle through. Insert the needle in the same hole. Bring it out directly above, in the second line at the end of the previous stitch. Take the thread under the needle point.

6 Pull the needle through. Take the needle to the back directly above, on the third line.

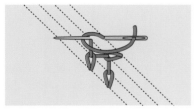

7 Bring the thread out on the top line, level with the top of the previous stitch. Insert the needle in the same hole, and bring it out to the left, on the third line. Take the thread under the needle point.

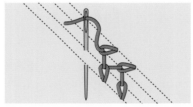

8 Pull the needle through. Insert the needle in the second line, level with where the thread emerged. Bring it out directly below, on the bottom line.

9 Continue in the same way to build up a line of stitching. Finish with a stitch to anchor the final chain.

10 Turn the work until the last stitch is at the bottom, for the final effect.

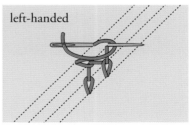

left-handed

❶ *Left-handers work this stitch in mirror image.*

crested chain stitch

This stitch is also known as *Spanish coral stitch*. It makes a pretty, decorative border.

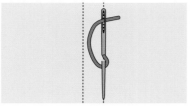

1 Use two guide lines. Bring the thread out on the right line. Make a very short chain stitch down the line.

2 Pull the needle through. Level with where the thread emerges, take a short stitch down the left line. Take the thread left over the needle and to the right under the needle point.

3 Pull the needle through to create a very small twisted chain/coral knot.

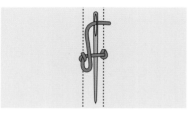

4 From above, slide the needle under the stitch that stretches from line to line.
❶ *Do not enter the fabric.*

5 Insert the needle into the tiny chain on the right line, bringing the needle out lower down the line. Take the thread under the needle point.

6 Pull the needle through.

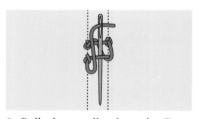

7 Level with where the thread emerges, take a short stitch down the left line. Take the thread to the left over the needle, then around under the needle point.

8 Pull the needle through. From above, slide the needle under the stitch that stretches from line to line.
❶ *Do not enter the fabric.*

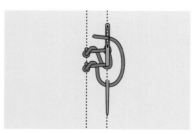

9 Insert the needle into the large chain on the right line. Using the same spacing as before, bring the needle out lower down the line. Take the thread under the needle point.

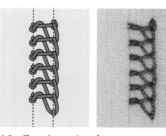

10 Continue in the same way, to build up a line of stitching. To finish, take a short stitch over the final chain on the right line.
❶ *Left-handers work this stitch in the same way.*

chevron stitch

Chevron stitch can be used as both a line and filling stitch. It does not work very successfully on curves.

1 Use two lines. Bring the needle out on the top line. A short way right, insert the needle in the line, bringing it out again halfway between. Keep the thread above the needle.

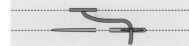

2 Pull the needle through. In the lower line, insert the needle half a stitch length along from the end of the first stitch. Bring it out level with the end of the first stitch.

3 Pull the needle through. Using the same length as before, insert the needle further along the line. Bring it out again halfway back. The thread sits below the needle.

4 Pull the needle through. In the top line, insert the needle half a stitch length along from the previous stitch's end. Bring it out level with the end.

5 Pull the needle through. Using the same length as before, insert the needle further along the line. Bring it out again halfway back. The thread should be above the needle.

6 Pull the needle through. In the lower line, insert the needle half a stitch length along from the previous stitch's end. Bring it out level with the end.

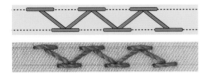

7 Continue in the same manner to build up a line of stitching.

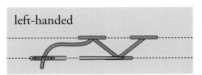

left-handed

❶ *Left-handers work this stitch in mirror image, travelling left.*

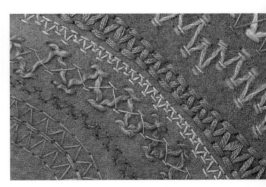

closed chevron stitch

This variation has no space between the horizontal stitches.

1 Use two lines. Bring the needle out on the top line. A short way right, insert the needle in the line, bringing it out again halfway between. Keep the thread above the needle.

2 Pull the needle through. Insert the needle in the lower line, level with the end of the first stitch. Bring it out level with the middle of that stitch.

3 Pull the needle through. Using the same length as for the first stitch, insert the needle further right along the line. Bring the needle out at the end of the diagonal stitch. Keep the thread below the needle.

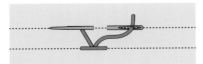

4 Pull the needle through. Insert the needle in the upper line, level with the end of the previous horizontal stitch. Bring it out level with the middle of that stitch.

5 Pull the needle through. Using the same length as before, insert the needle further along the line. Bring the needle out at the end of the diagonal stitch. Keep the thread above the needle.

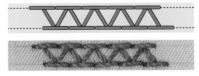

6 Continue in the same manner to build up a line of stitching.
❶ *As for regular chevron stitch, left-handers work this stitch in mirror image, travelling left.*

pagoda chevron stitch

In this variation, the stitches emerge on the outside of the straight stitch, rather than the inner side.

1 Use two lines. Bring the needle out on the top line. A short way right, insert the needle in the line, bringing it out again halfway between. Keep the thread below the needle.

2 Pull the needle through. In the lower line, moving right, insert the needle half a stitch length along from the end of the first stitch. Bring it out level with the end of the first stitch.

3 Pull the needle through. With the same stitch length as before, insert the needle further along the line. Bring it out again halfway back. The thread sits above the needle.

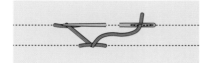

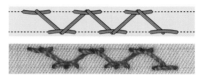

4 Pull the needle through. In the top line, insert the needle half a stitch length along from the previous stitch's end. Bring it out level with that.

5 Pull the needle through. Insert the needle further along the line. Bring it out again halfway back. The thread sits below the needle.

6 Continue in the same manner to build up a line of stitching.

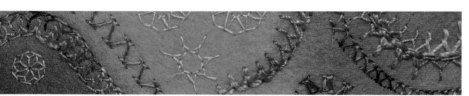

left-handed

❶ *Left-handers work this stitch in mirror image, travelling left.*

half chevron stitch

The top half of this stitch is a Cretan stitch, and the bottom half is a closed chevron stitch.

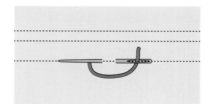

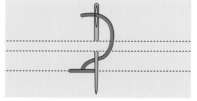

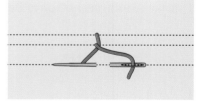

1 Use three lines. Bring the needle out on the bottom line. Insert the needle in the line, a stitch length to the right. Bring it out halfway between. Keep the thread below the needle.

2 Pull the needle through. Level with the end of the first stitch, vertically insert the needle in the top line. Bring it out on the middle line. The thread goes under the needle point.

3 Pull the needle through. Insert the needle in the bottom line, half a stitch length along from the end of the first stitch. Bring it out at the end of the first stitch.

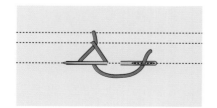

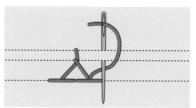

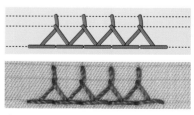

4 Pull the needle through. Insert the needle, a stitch length to the right. Bring it out at the end of the first stitch. Keep the thread below the needle.

5 Pull the needle through. Take a vertical stitch from the top to the middle line. The thread goes under the needle point.

6 Continue in the same way to build up a line of stitching.
❶ *Left-handers work this stitch in mirror image, travelling left.*

raised chevron stitch

Raised chevron stitch is chevron stitch worked on a foundation of 'v'-shaped stitches. The foundation and the chevron stitches can be worked in the same or contrasting colours.

1 Use a line of joined diamonds as guides. Bring the needle out on the left corner of the left-most diamond. Take a stitch from the bottom of that diamond to the bottom of the next.

2 Pull the needle through. Take a stitch from the right to the left corners of the second diamond along.

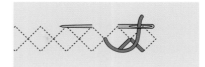

3 Pull the needle through. Take a stitch from the top of the second diamond to the top of the third diamond.

4 Pull the needle through. Take a stitch from the right to the left corners of the third diamond.

5 Pull the needle through. Take a stitch from the bottom of the third diamond to the bottom of the fourth diamond.

6 Continue in the same way to build up a framework of stitches, ready for working the chevron stitches.

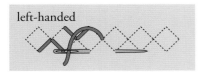

❶ *Left-handers work the foundation stitches in mirror image, from left to right.*

7 Change to a tapestry needle. Bring a new thread out just left of the 'v' at the left end. With the thread above the needle, slide it under the left half of the 'v', from the right.

❶ *Do not enter the fabric during the chevron stitching.*

8 Slide the needle under the right half of the 'v', from right to left. Take the thread under the needle point.

9 Slide the needle under the left half of the next 'v', from right to left. Keep the thread below the needle.

10 With the thread above the needle, slide it under the right half of the 'v', from the right.

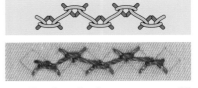

11 Continue in the same way to fill all the foundation stitches.

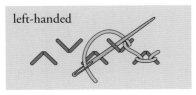

❶ *Left-handers work the chevron stitches in mirror image.*

chinese knot

Chinese knots are similar to French knots, but have a small stalk, which French knots don't have. They can be used in a line, or singly. Also known as *Pekin knot*.

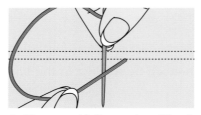

1 Use two guide lines and a milliner's needle. Bring the thread out on the lower line. Lay it over the needle.

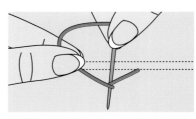

2 Take the thread towards the right behind the needle, then across the front, to wrap it once.

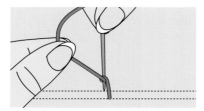

3 Hold the thread upwards, and move the needle up and right, making sure the wrap remains on the needle.

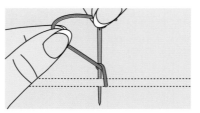

4 Just left of the emerging thread, vertically insert the needle from the upper to the lower line.

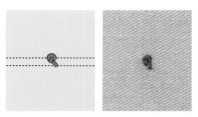

❶ *To work a single knot, at step 4, insert the needle in the upper line, take the thread through to the back, and tighten the knot.*

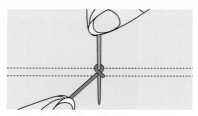

5 Pull the thread downwards to tighten the thread so that it is snug around the needle.

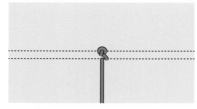

6 Pull the needle through.

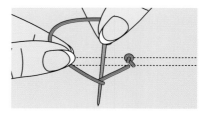

7 Take the thread across the needle and wrap it once as before.

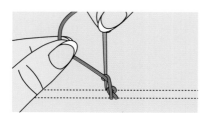

8 Hold the thread upwards, and move the needle up and right, making sure the wrap remains on the needle.

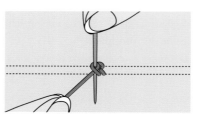

9 The same distance to the left as before, insert the needle from the upper to the lower line. Tighten the stitch around the needle.

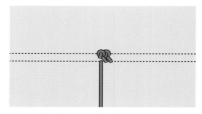

10 Pull the needle through.

11 Continue in the same way to build up a line of stitching.

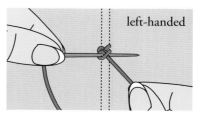

left-handed

❶ *Left-handers work this stitch turned 90 degrees anticlockwise, inserting the needle from left to right.*

colonial knot

This stitch is also sometimes called *figure of eight knot* because the thread wraps around the needle in the shape of an '8'. It is commonly used in contemporary candlewick embroidery.

1 Bring the thread out where the knot is required. Holding the thread in the left hand, place the needle over the top, with the point towards where the thread emerged.

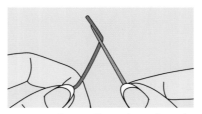

2 Move the needle to the right, taking the needle point under the top part of the thread.

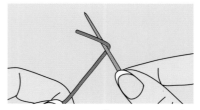

3 Bring the needle across to the right, with the needle point under the thread.

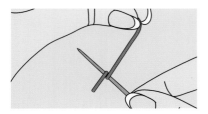

4 Lift your left hand up.
❶ *The thread is now wrapped around the needle.*

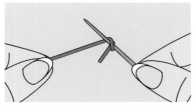

5 Take the thread down behind the needle point, from right to left.

6 Pull the thread down, and ensure that the knot is snug around the shaft of the needle.

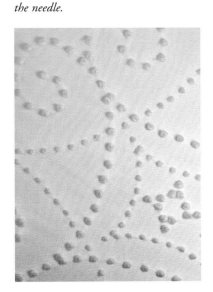

7 Insert the needle next to where the thread emerges from the fabric.

8 Gently pull the thread to tighten the knot on the surface of the fabric.

9 Take the needle and thread through to the back to complete the knot.

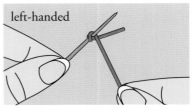

left-handed

❶ *Left-handers work this stitch in mirror image.*

coral knot stitch

When the knots of this stitch are worked extremely close together the stitch can look like a tightly twisted cord. When spaced further apart, the line looks like a thread punctuated by little knots. Sometimes known as *coral stitch*.

1 Bring the thread out on the line. Diagonally insert the needle just right of the line, and bring it out just left of the line a short way above.
❶ *The needle should go under only a few threads to keep the stitch very short.*

2 Lay the thread along the line.
❶ *Doing this helps to check that the thread is wrapping the correct way around the needle. Wrapping the other way makes a different stitch.*

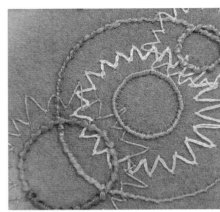

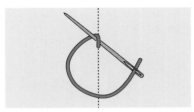

3 Take the thread down behind the needle from right to left.

4 Pull the needle through and tighten to create a small knot.
❶ *If the stitch taken at step 1 is too long, the knot will not be small.*

5 A short way to the above, insert the needle just right of the line using the same stitch length and angle as before.

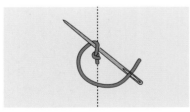

6 Take the thread along the line, and down behind the needle point.

7 Pull the needle through and tighten to create a small knot.

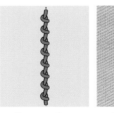

8 Repeat the steps to build up a line of knots. To finish, take the thread to the back after the final knot.

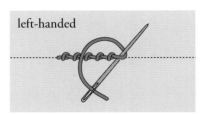

left-handed

❶ *Left-handers work this stitch turned 90 degrees clockwise.*

In some embroidery styles such as Schwalm embroidery from Germany, the knots are worked with the needle perpendicular to the line, rather than on an angle.

zigzagging coral knot stitch

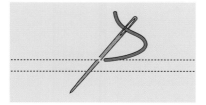

1 Bring the thread out on the upper line. Diagonally insert the needle just above the line, and bring it out just below the line a very short way to the left.

❶ *The needle goes under only a few threads so that the stitch is very short.*

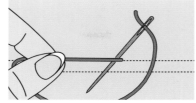

2 Lay the thread along the line.

❶ *Doing this helps to check that the thread is wrapping the correct way around the needle. Wrapping the other way makes a different stitch.*

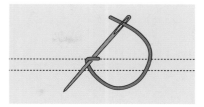

3 Take the thread down behind the needle from left to right.

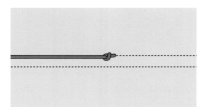

4 Pull the needle through and tighten to create a small knot.

❶ *If the stitch taken at step 1 is too long, the knot will not be small.*

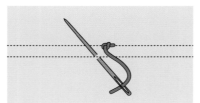

5 A short way to the left, insert the needle the lower line diagonally from below, using the same stitch length as before.

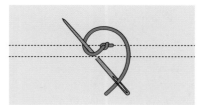

6 Take the thread down across the front of the needle and up behind the needle point.

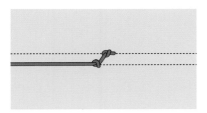

7 Pull the needle through and tighten to create a small knot.

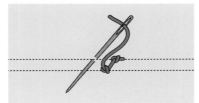

8 From above, make a stitch in the top line, using the same angle and stitch length as for the first stitch.

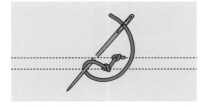

9 Take the thread up across the front of the needle and down behind the needle point.

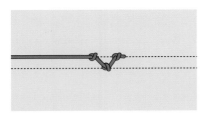

10 Pull the needle through, and tighten to create a small knot.

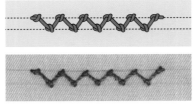

11 Keep working knots on alternate lines to build up a line of stitching. To finish, take the thread to the back after the final stitch.

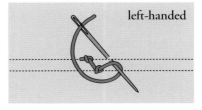

left-handed

❶ *Left-handers work this stitch in mirror image from left to right.*

couching

Couching can be used as an outline or filling stitch. Any number of threads can be couched.

1 Use one guide. Bring the threads to be couched (the laid threads) out on the guide line. Lay them flat along the line.

2 Hold the laid threads in place. Bring a new thread out below the laid threads near their beginning. Take a short stitch over the laid threads, and bring the needle out further to the left, below the laid threads.

3 Repeat to build up a line of couching.

❶ *The laid threads should not pucker or be too loose, but should lie flat against the fabric.*

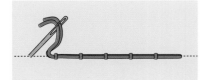

4 When the line of couching is complete, thread the laid threads into a needle and take them to the back of the fabric and secure.

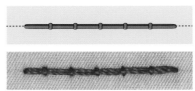

5 The completed couching.

❶ *Couching can also be used as a filling stitch by turning the laid threads at the edges of the shape and couching them next to the previous row.*

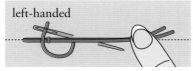

left-handed

❶ *Left-handers work this stitch in mirror image, from left to right.*

couched trellis

Couched trellis is created by laying threads and couching them with either half crosses or cross stitch.

1 Using even spacing, work parallel stitches back and forth across the shape.

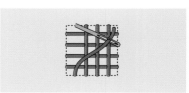

2 Work stitches up and down to fill the shape, with the same spacing.

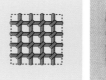

3 Over the intersections of the laid stitches, work a half cross.

❶ *All couching stitches lie in the same direction.*

❶ *Work a full cross over each intersection, so that all the top stitches lie in the same direction.*

couched burden stitch

There are two Burden stitches: one is couched the other is a running stitch (see page 130). This couched version originated in Middle Ages ecclesiastical work and is named after needlework teacher Elizabeth Burden, who popularised it in the late 1800s. The laid and couching stitches can be the same or contrasting colours.

1 Take a long stitch across the fabric.

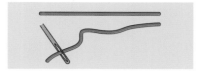

2 Pull the needle through. Bring the needle out below the right end of the stitch. Take the needle through to the back below its left end.

3 Continue stitching back and forth across, with long stitches.
❶ *These are the laid stitches that will be couched down.*

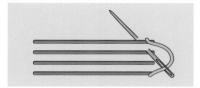

4 Bring a new thread out just above the top stitch, at the right end. Directly down, insert the thread just above the second laid stitch, bringing it out a little to the left, just above the top stitch.

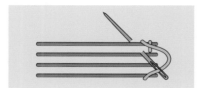

5 Pull the needle through. Using the same spacing, insert the needle from just above the second laid stitch, to just above the first.
❶ *The ends of the couching stitches should touch the second laid stitch.*

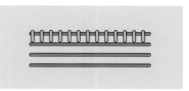

6 Continue working evenly spaced stitches to fill the row.

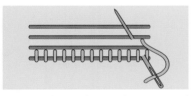

7 Turn the work 180 degrees to aid insertion of the needle. Bring the needle out below the second laid stitch, between the first two stitches of the first row. Using the same spacing as before, take a stitch over the third laid stitch, between the second and fourth laid stitches.

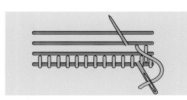

8 Pull the needle through. Moving to the left along the row, take another stitch.
❶ *The ends of the couching stitches touch the laid stitches above and below.*

9 Continue working evenly spaced stitches to fill the row.

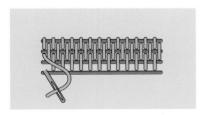

10 Turn the work 180 degrees again, and work stitches stretching between the laid stitches, to fill the next row down.

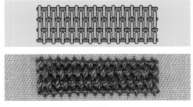

11 Continue filling rows as required. The last row is worked similarly to the first, so that stitches end just over the outermost laid stitch.

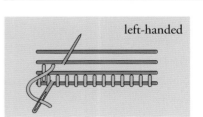

left-handed

❶ *Left-handers work this stitch in mirror image, travelling from left to right.*

bokhara couching

Bokhara couching is a self-couched stitch in which each stitch is laid and then with the same thread, couched a number of times, to form a pattern.

1 Use two wide-set guides. Bring the thread out on the left line. Level with that, insert the needle in the right line, bringing it out a little way along and just a little down. The thread sits above the needle.

2 Pull the needle through, so that there is a straight stitch (the laid stitch) with the thread emerging just below it.

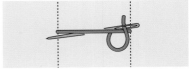

3 A short way along, insert the needle above the thread, and using the same stitch length as before, take another diagonal stitch, emerging just below the thread.

4 Pull the needle through. Using the same spacing as before, insert the needle above the thread. Bring it out just below the end of the previous stitch, ready for laying the next thread.

5 Pull the needle through.
❶ *The laid stitch has very short couching stitches crossing it at regular intervals.*

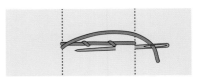

6 Level with the emerging thread, insert the needle in the right line, bringing it out level with the first couching stitch. The thread sits above the needle.

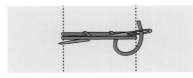

7 Pull the needle through. Using the same spacing and stitch length as before insert the needle between the two laid stitches, emerging further on, just below the current laid stitch.

8 Pull the needle through. Using the same spacing between stitches as before, insert the needle between the two laid stitches. Bring it out just below the end of the laid stitch, ready for laying the next thread.

9 Pull the needle through.

10 Continue in the same way to build up a shape filled with Bokhara couching.

❶ *Patterns can be made with the placement of the couching stitches. Here, every second laid stitch has its couching stitches sitting between those of the previous row.*

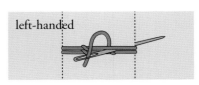

left-handed

❶ *Left-handers work this stitch rotated 180 degrees, from bottom to top.*

roumanian couching

This stitch is similar to Bokhara couching. Instead of multiple couching stitches for each laid stitch (as in Bokhara), there is a single central row of couching stitches.

Roumanian couching is also called *Roman stitch*, *oriental stitch*, *laid oriental stitch*, *figure stitch*, *antique stitch*, *Indian filling stitch*, and *Janina stitch*.

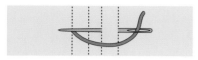

1 Use four guides, with two closer together in the middle. Bring the thread out on the left line. Level with that, take a stitch from the right line to the next closest one. The thread goes below the needle.

2 Pull the needle through, so that there is a straight stitch (the laid stitch) with the thread emerging above the line.

3 Push the laid stitch up and insert the needle directly underneath where it would sit, in the third line from the right. Bring it out below the first stitch in the left line.

4 Pull the needle through.
❶ *The laid and the couched stitches intertwine.*

5 Level with the emerging thread, take a stitch from the right line to the next closest one. The thread goes below the needle.

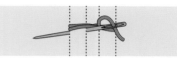

6 Pull the needle through. Push the laid stitch up and insert the needle in the third line across. Bring it out below the previous stitch in the left line.

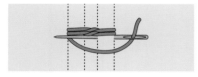

7 Pull the needle through. Just below the previous stitch, take a stitch from the right line to the next closest one. The thread goes below the needle.

8 Continue in the same way to build up a line of stitches.

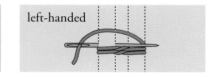

❶ *Left-handers work this stitch rotated 180 degrees, from bottom to top.*

new england laid stitch

From Deerfield embroidery, New England laid stitch is a variation of Roumanian couching, but has much longer couching stitches.

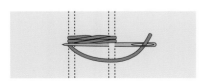

The couching stitches are almost as long as the laid stitch, providing very full coverage on the front of the fabric, and very little thread on the back.

The laid and couching stitches of New England laid stitch blend together so that it is difficult to distinguish separate stitches.

Working the stitches spaced apart creates open New England laid stitch.

cretan stitch

Cretan stitch is closely related to feather stitch. By varying stitch length and spacing different effects are obtained.

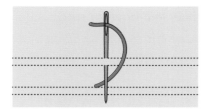

1 Use four guides. Bring the thread out on the third line down. A little right, vertically insert the needle from the top line to the line below. Take the needle point over the thread.

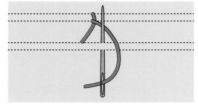

2 Pull the needle through. Using the same spacing as previously, vertically insert the needle from the bottom line to the line above. Take the needle point over the thread.

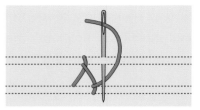

3 Pull the needle through. A little right, vertically insert the needle from the top line to the one below. Take the needle point over the thread.

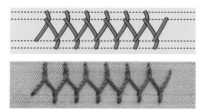

4 Continue to build up a line of stitching. To finish, take the thread to the back on one of the inner two lines.

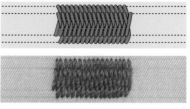

❶ *For closed Cretan stitch, work the stitches very close together.*

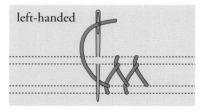

left-handed

❶ *Left-handers work this stitch in mirror image, from right to left.*

cretan catch stitch

This stitch has Cretan stitch at the top and herringbone at the bottom.

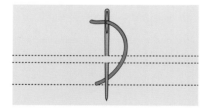

1 Use three guides. Bring the thread out on the bottom line. A little to the right, vertically insert the needle from the top line to the line below. Take the needle point over the thread.

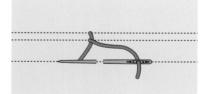

2 Pull the needle through. A little way to the right, insert the needle from right to left in the bottom line. Take a short stitch.

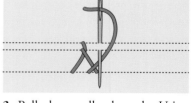

3 Pull the needle through. Using the same distance as before, vertically insert the needle from the top line to the line below. Take the needle point over the thread.

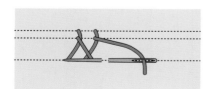

4 Pull the needle through. Using the same spacing and stitch length as before, make a stitch in the bottom line from right to left.

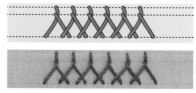

5 Continue working Cretan and herringbone stitches to build up a line of stitching. To finish, take the thread to the back on the bottom line.

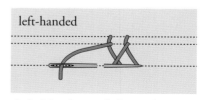

left-handed

❶ *Left-handers work this stitch in mirror image, from right to left.*

knotted cretan stitch

Unlike regular Cretan stitch, this variation is worked from left to right as it aids inserting the needle with ease for the knotted stitch.

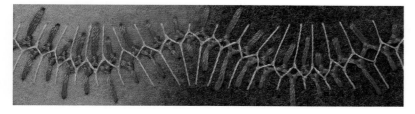

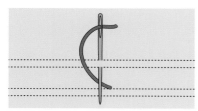

1 Use four guide lines. Bring the thread out on the third line down. A little to the left, vertically insert the needle in the top line and bring it out on the line below. Take the needle point over the thread.

2 Pull the needle through. From the right, slide the needle under the part of the previous stitch below where the thread emerges. Take the thread under the needle point.
❶ *Do not enter the fabric.*

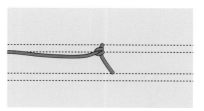

3 Pull the needle through, and gently tighten the knot.
❶ *The knot is actually a tiny chain stitch.*

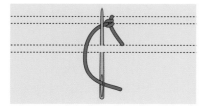

4 Moving left again, from below insert the needle vertically in the bottom line, bringing it out in the line above. Take the needle point over the thread.

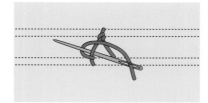

5 Pull the needle through. From the right, slide the needle under the part of the previous stitch above where the thread emerges. Take the thread under the needle point.
❶ *Do not enter the fabric.*

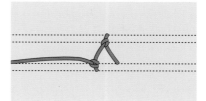

6 Pull the needle through, and gently tighten the knot.

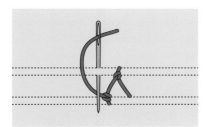

7 A little to the left, vertically insert the needle in the top line and bring it out on the line below. Take the needle point over the thread.

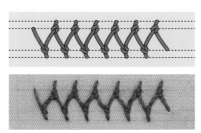

8 Continue in the same manner, to build up a line of stitching.

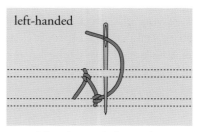
left-handed

❶ *Left-handers work this stitch in mirror image, from left to right.*

71

cross stitch

Cross stitch can be worked counted on evenweave fabric or canvas, or freestyle as surface embroidery. Also known as *Berlin stitch*, *gros point*, *point de marque* and *sampler stitch*.

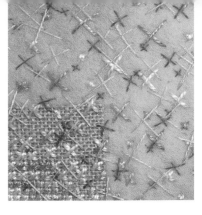

full cross (English) method

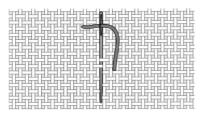

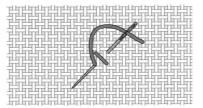

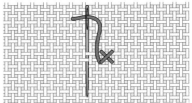

1 Using a tapestry needle, bring the thread out. Insert the needle two threads left and up. Bring it out down two threads.

2 Pull the needle through. Insert it two threads right and up. Bring it out where the thread emerged.
❶ *To work a single cross, take the thread to the back and fasten it.*

3 Pull the needle through. Insert the needle two threads left and up. Bring it out down two threads.

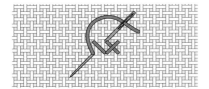

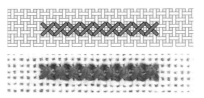

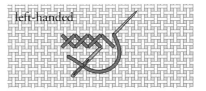
left-handed

4 Pull the needle through. Insert it two threads right and up. Bring it out where the thread emerged.

5 Continue in the same way to build up a line of stitching.
❶ *The top stitches should always lie in the same orientation.*

❶ *Left-handers work this stitch turned 180 degrees.*

half cross (Danish) method

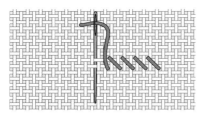

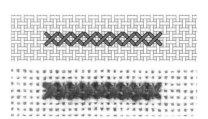

1 Work a half cross as in the first step above. Pull the needle through. Continue inserting it two threads left and up, then bringing it out down two.
❶ *Stopping here makes half cross stitch.*

2 When all the half crosses are stitched, work back towards the beginning. Insert the needle two threads right and up. Bring it out down two threads.

3 Continue right in the same way to cross all remaining half crosses.
❶ *Left-handers work this method in the same way.*

using variegated threads

Different effects can be obtained when using variegated threads depending on the method used.

With the full cross method, the colour gradually changes across the row, with obvious distinct colours.

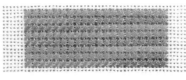

With the half cross method, the different shades mix across the rows giving a more homogeneous effect.

smyrna cross stitch

Also known as *double cross*, *leviathan stitch* and *railway stitch*. When used used as a counted thread stitch, it can be worked over any multiple of two threads.

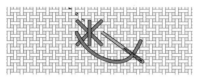

1 Using a tapestry needle, bring the thread out. Insert the needle four threads down and right, bringing it out four threads to the left.

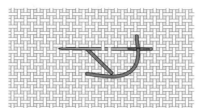

2 Pull the needle through. Insert it four threads up and right. Bring the needle out two threads left, in the middle of the top edge.

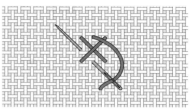

3 Pull the needle through. Insert the needle in the middle of the bottom, bringing it out at the middle of the left side.

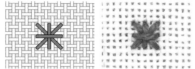

4 Pull the needle through. Take the needle through to the back in the middle of the right side.

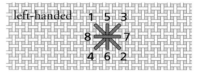

5 The completed Smyrna cross.

left-handed

❶ *Left-handers work the sequence shown, coming out at the odd numbers, and going in at the even numbers.*

chained cross stitch

This cross stitch has a chain instead of the top crossing stitch. Each cross is fully worked before moving on to the next one.

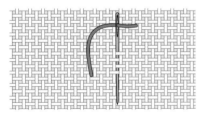

1 Using a tapestry needle, bring the thread out. Insert the needle four threads above and right. Bring it out four threads below.

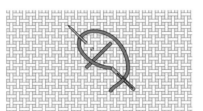

2 Pull the needle through. Insert it where the thread emerges. Bring it out four threads up and left. Take the thread under the needle point.

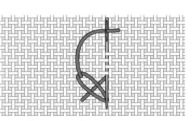

3 Pull the needle through. Insert it four threads up and right. Bring it out four threads below, at the end of the half cross.

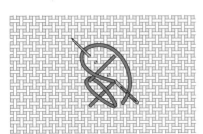

4 Pull the needle through. Diagonally insert the needle where the thread emerges. Bring it four threads up and left. Take the thread under the needle point.

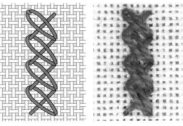

5 Pull the needle through to create a chain stitch. Continue in the same manner to build up a line of stitching. Finish with a short anchor stitch over the final chain.

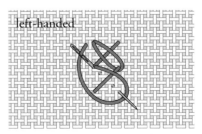

left-handed

❶ *Left-handers work this stitch turned 180 degrees, from top to bottom.*

plaited cross stitch

Also known as *woven cross stitch*, this stitch is similar to a small Norwich stitch. Use a tapestry needle.

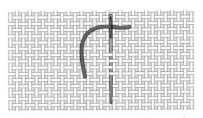

1 Bring the thread out. Insert the needle four threads up and right, bringing it out four threads below.

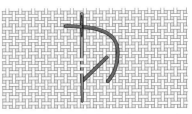

2 Pull the needle through. Insert the needle four threads up and left, bringing it out three threads below.

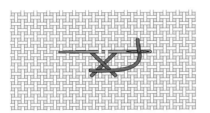

3 Pull the needle through. Insert it three threads up and right, bringing it out two threads left.

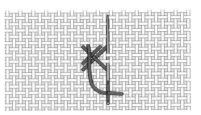

4 Pull the needle through. Insert it three threads down and right, bringing it out two threads up.

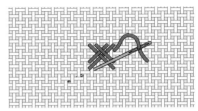

5 Pull the needle through. Take the needle to the back three threads down and left.

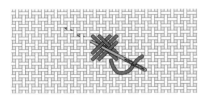

6 Bring the needle out two threads right. Take it under the uppermost left crossing stitch and insert it three threads up and left.

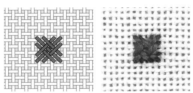

7 The completed plaited cross stitch.

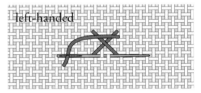

❶ *Left-handers work this stitch turned 180 degrees.*

sofia stitch

This stitch has three crosses one on top of the other to create a star shape. Use a tapestry needle.

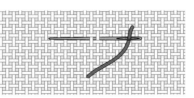

1 Bring the needle out. Insert it six threads up and two right. Bring it out two threads to the left.

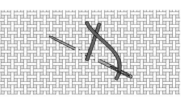

2 Pull the needle through. Insert it six threads down and two right. Bring it out two up and four left.

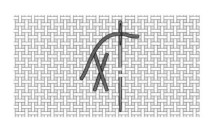

3 Pull the needle through. Insert it two threads up and six right. Bring the needle out two threads down.

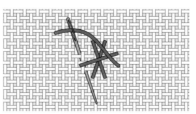

4 Pull the needle through. Insert it six threads left and two up. Bring it out three down and one right.

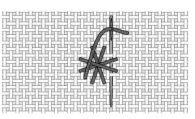

5 Pull the needle through. Insert it four threads up and right. Bring it out four threads down.

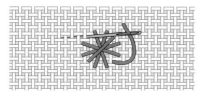

6 Pull the needle through. Take it to the back four threads up and left.

7 The completed Sofia stitch.

❶ *Left-handers work this stitch turned 180 degrees.*

long-legged cross stitch

This stitch looks similar to herringbone stitch but is worked differently. Also known as *long-armed cross stitch*, *plaited Slav stitch*, *Portuguese stitch* and *twist stitch*. Use a tapestry needle.

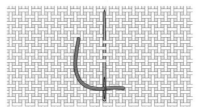

1 Bring the thread out. Insert the needle four threads down and right, bringing it out four threads above.

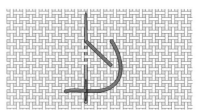

2 Pull the needle through. Insert the needle four threads down and left, bringing it out four threads above.

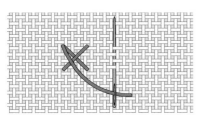

3 Pull the needle through. Insert it four threads down and eight threads right. Bring it out four threads up.

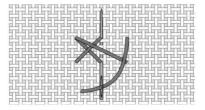

4 Pull the needle through. Insert the needle four threads down and left, bringing it out four threads above.

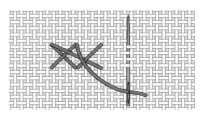

5 Pull the needle through. Insert the needle four threads down and eight to the right. Bring it out four threads up.

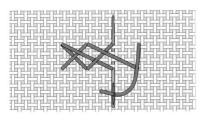

6 Pull the needle through. Insert the needle four threads down and left, bringing it out four threads above.

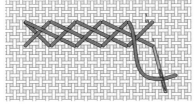

7 Continue similarly. To finish, take the thread to the back at the bottom end of a long stitch, as shown.

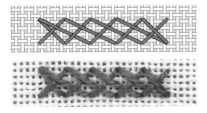

8 The completed stitch.
❶ *Left-handers work this stitch in exactly the same way.*

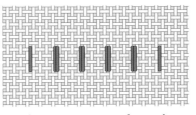

❶ *The reverse is a series of vertical stitches. Though herringbone is similar, its reverse has two lines of back stitch.*

italian two-sided cross stitch

This reversible stitch is also known as *arrowhead stitch*, *Italian cross stitch*, and *two-sided Italian stitch*.

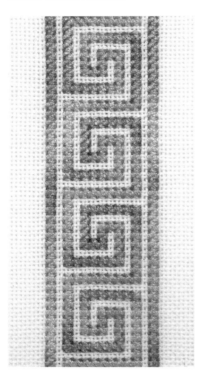

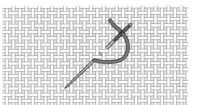

1 Using a tapestry needle, bring the thread out. Insert the needle two threads up and right, bringing it out where the thread emerged.

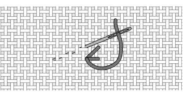

3 Pull the needle through. Take the needle to the back two threads above.

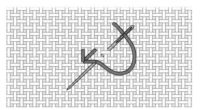

5 Pull the needle through. Insert the needle two threads up and right, bringing it out where the thread emerged.

7 Pull the needle through. Take the needle to the back two threads above.

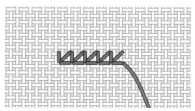

9 Continue in the same way to build up a line of stitching, ready for the return journey.

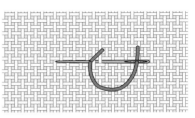

2 Pull the needle through. Insert the needle two threads to the right, bringing it out in the same place as before.

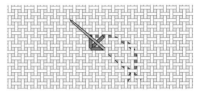

4 Bring the needle out two threads down and right.

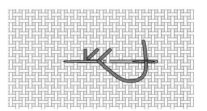

6 Pull the needle through. Insert the needle two threads right, bringing it out in the same place as before.

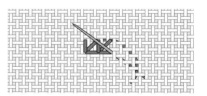

8 Bring the needle out two threads down and right.

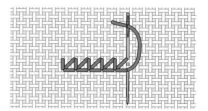

10 Insert the needle two threads above, bringing it out in where the thread emerged.

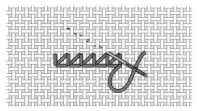

11 Pull the needle through. Take the needle to the back two threads up and left.

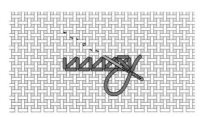

14 Pull the needle through. Take the needle to the back two threads up and left.

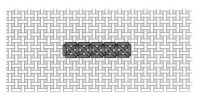

17 Continue working in the same manner to complete the rest of the row.

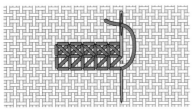

20 Insert the needle two threads above, bringing it out where the thread emerged.

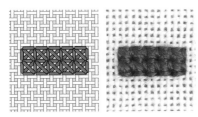

23 Continue in the same way to complete the row.

❶ *This stitch can also be worked as a pulled thread stitch, by gently tightening the thread after each stitch.*

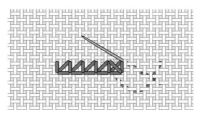

12 Bring the needle out two threads to the right.

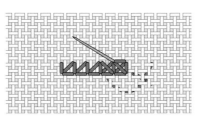

15 Bring the needle out two threads to the right.

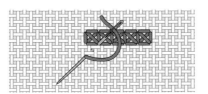

18 Bring the needle out two threads below the first row. Insert it two threads up and right. Bring it out where the thread emerged.

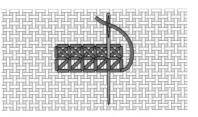

21 Pull the needle through. Insert the needle two threads up and left. Bring it out two threads below.

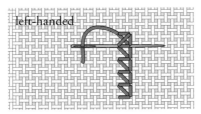

left-handed

❶ *Left-handers work this stitch turned 90 degrees anticlockwise.*

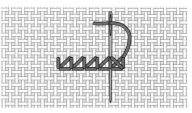

13 Pull the needle through. Insert the needle two threads to the left, bringing it out two threads below.

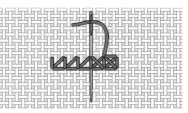

16 Pull the needle through. Insert the needle two threads to the left, bringing it out two threads below.

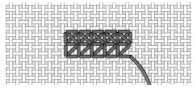

19 Complete the rest of the row, using the same method as for the first row's outward journey.

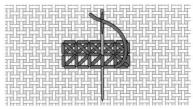

22 Pull the needle through. Insert the needle two threads up and left. Bring it out two threads below.

rice stitch

Also known as *crossed corners stitch, crossed corners cross stitch* and *William and Mary stitch*. Use a tapestry needle.

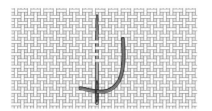

1 Bring the thread out. Insert the needle four threads left and below, bringing it out four threads above.

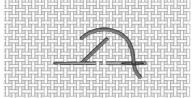

2 Pull the needle through. Insert it four threads right and down. Bring it in the middle of the bottom side.

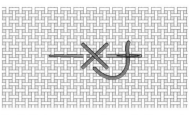

3 Pull the needle through. Insert it in the middle of the right, bringing it out in the middle of the left side.

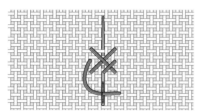

4 Pull the needle through. Insert it in the bottom middle. Bring it out in the middle of the top side.

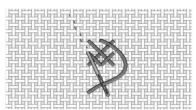

5 Pull the needle through. Take the needle to the back in the middle of the left side.

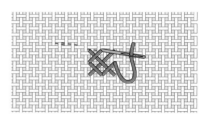

6 Pull the needle through. Bring it out in the middle right. Take the thread to the back in the middle top.

7 The completed rice stitch.

❶ *Left-handers work this stitch in mirror image.*

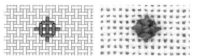

❶ *When worked turned 45 degrees, it is called diagonal rice stitch.*

as a filling stitch

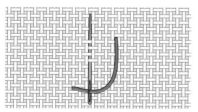

1 Bring the thread out. Insert the needle four threads left and below, bringing it out four threads above.

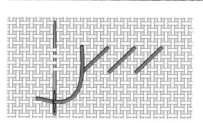

2 Moving left, continue working half crosses to fill the required space.

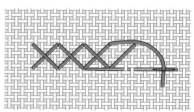

3 Work back to complete the crosses. Bring the needle out in the bottom middle.

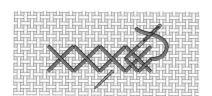

4 In the same way as above, cross the first cross's corners. Bring the needle out centre bottom of the next cross.

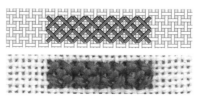

5 Continue in the same way to cross the corners of the entire row.

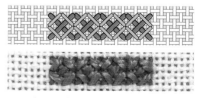

❶ *The two layers can be worked in different colours and thicknesses of thread.*

diamond stitch

This is a very pretty border stitch. Use careful, even tension throughout. For curves, gentle curves are best.

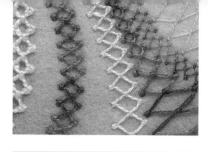

1 Use two guides. Bring the needle out on the right line. Level with that, take it to the back on the left line.

2 Bring the thread out just below where it first emerged. From above, slide the needle under the first stitch's right end, but do not enter the fabric. Take the thread left over the needle front and up behind the needle point.

3 Pull the needle downwards, to tighten the stitch into a small knot, close to the right line.

❶ *Ensure the knot sits as close as possible to the right line.*

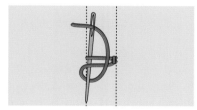 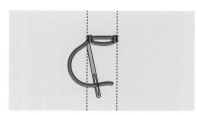 

4 Insert the needle under the left end of the first stitch from above, but do not enter the fabric. Take the thread left over the front of the needle and up behind the needle point.

5 Pull the needle through to the left, to tighten the knot as close as possible to the left line. Take the thread to the back just under the knot.

❶ *The thread between the knots should hang down in a gentle curve.*

6 Bring the needle out on the left line a little way down. Insert the needle under the gently curving stitch, from above. Take the thread across and down behind the needle point.

❶ *Do not enter the fabric.*

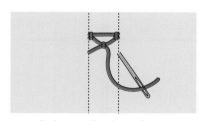  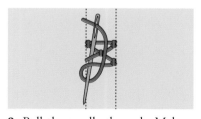

7 Pull the needle through, tightening the knot in the centre of the previous stitch. Take the needle through to the back on the right line, level with where it emerged on the left.

8 Bring the needle out on the right line, just below. Make a knot at the right edge, in the previous stitch.

9 Pull the needle through. Make a knot at the left edge of the previous stitch, keeping the tension of the thread between the knots the same as before.

  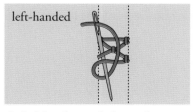

10 Using the same spacing, bring the needle out on the left line. Make a knot in the centre of the previous stitch.

11 Continue in the same manner to build up a line of stitching. Finish with the stitch that goes from right to left.

left-handed

❶ *Left-handers work this stitch in basically the same way, except they angle the needle more from the left instead of from the right.*

diamond upright stitch

This is a reversible stitch which forms a diagonal line of diamonds with crosses in their centres. Use a tapestry needle.

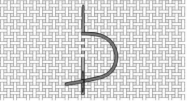

1 Bring the needle out of the fabric. Insert it four threads above, bringing it out where the thread emerged.

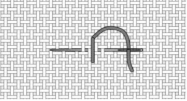

2 Pull the needle through. Insert the needle two threads down and right. Bring it out four threads to the left.

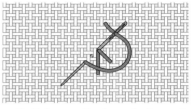

3 Pull the needle through. Insert it two threads up and right. Bring it out where the thread emerged.

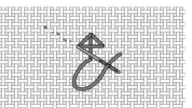

4 Pull the needle through. Insert it four threads right and bring it out again two threads left and down.

5 Pull the needle through. Take the thread to the back two threads up and left.

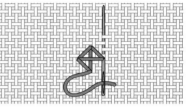

6 Bring the thread out again two threads down and right. Insert the needle two threads right and up. Bring it out four threads further up.

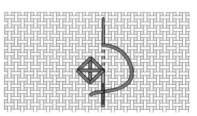

7 Pull the needle through. Insert it four threads below, bringing it out where the thread emerged.

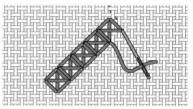

8 Cycle through steps 2 to 7 to build up a line of stitching. To finish, take the thread to the back at step 6.

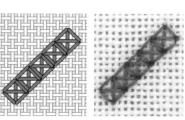

9 The completed diamond upright stitch.

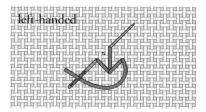

left-handed

❶ *Left-handers work this stitch rotated 180 degrees, travelling up and right.*

drizzle stitch

Drizzle stitch is a Brazilian embroidery stitch, made of cast on stitches. It is best worked with a milliner's needle or for thicker threads, a darner needle.

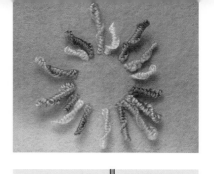

1 Bring the thread out of the fabric. Unthread the needle and insert it in the same hole as where the thread emerges.

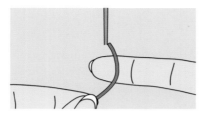

2 Place your right forefinger under the thread, with the underside of your finger facing you. Hold the thread in your left hand, to maintain a level of tension.

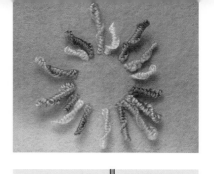

3 Keeping the thread on your finger, begin to turn your finger towards you, maintaining the tension with your left hand.

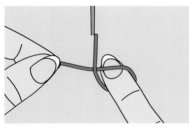

4 Keep turning until your finger is nail up.

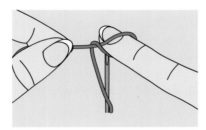

5 Lift your finger up onto the top of the needle.

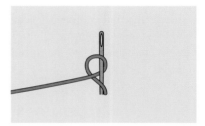

6 Tip your finger up so that the thread slides off your finger and onto the needle.

7 Pull the thread downwards to tighten it around the needle shaft.

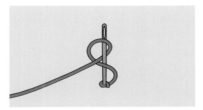

8 Using the same method, place another loop on the needle.

9 Tighten the loop around the base of the needle, so that it sits on top of the previous one.

10 Continue adding loops until there are as many as are required.

11 Rethread the needle, and gently holding the stitches on the needle, pull the needle and thread through.

12 The completed drizzle stitch.
❶ *Left-handers work this stitch in the same way.*

eyelets

This method makes tiny eyelets, which are small bound-edge holes in the fabric.

1 Running stitch around the guide, with short stitches and only going under a few fabric threads each time, so that most of the thread lies on top of the fabric.

2 Complete the running stitch around the circle. Leave the thread hanging from the front.

3 Pierce a hole in the centre of the circle with an awl, bodkin or stiletto.

4 Insert the needle in the hole, bringing it out just outside the running stitch, below where the thread emerged.

5 Pull the needle through and gently tighten the stitch. Moving anticlockwise around the circle, make a new stitch right next to the first.
❶ *Tightening the stitch enlarges the hole.*

6 Pull the needle through, tightening the stitch. Continue overcasting around the circle, turning the work as necessary to aid with insertion of the needle.

7 To finish, take the needle through to the back through the hole at the conclusion of the final stitch.

8 On the back of the eyelet, take the needle under the back of a few of the stitches, then trim the thread.
❶ *Use a thinner needle if it is difficult.*

left-handed

❶ *Left-handers work this stitch in mirror image.*

cut eyelets

These eyelets are cut rather than pierced, and can be any shape, including oval, triangular and square.

1 Work around the guide in running stitch, taking short stitches and only going under minimal fabric, so that most of the thread lies on top of the fabric.

2 Complete the running stitched circle. Leave the thread hanging from the front. Using sharp embroidery scissors, make a number of cuts from the centre, to near the edge, taking care to not cut the stitches.

3 Fold the flaps of fabric to the back.

4 Insert the needle in the hole, bringing it out just outside the running stitch, below where the thread emerged.

5 Pull the needle through and gently tighten the stitch. Moving anti-clockwise around the circle, make a new stitch right next to the first.
❶ *Tightening the stitch enlarges the hole.*

6 Continue overcasting around the circle, turning the work as necessary to aid with insertion of the needle. To finish, take the needle through to the back through the hole at the conclusion of the final stitch.

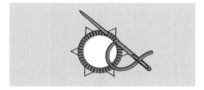  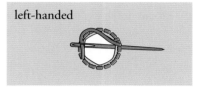

7 On the back of the eyelet, take the needle under the back of a few of the stitches, then trim the thread.
❶ *Use a thinner needle if it is difficult.*

8 On the back, trim away the excess fabric with small, sharp scissors.

❶ *Left-handers work this stitch in mirror image.*

counted eyelets

These eyelets are a pulled thread stitch usually worked over blocks of four by four threads, to create a small hole in the fabric. They are used extensively in Hardanger embroidery. Use a tapestry needle.

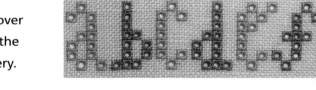

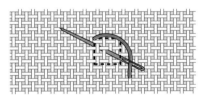 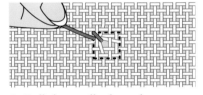 

1 Bring the thread out in the top left corner of a block of four by four threads. Insert the needle in the centre of the block, bringing it out again one thread below where the thread emerged.
❶ *Always insert the needle at the eyelet centre and bring it out at the edge.*

2 Pull the needle through.
❶ *After each stitch gently pull the thread away from the centre to tighten the stitch and enlarge the centre hole. Even tension throughout creates a regular shaped hole.*

3 Insert the needle in the centre. Bring it out again one thread below the previous stitch.

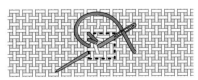  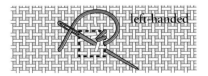

4 Pull the needle through and gently tighten the stitch. Insert the needle in the centre. Bring it out again one thread below the previous stitch.

5 Continue in the same way to work all the stitches around each side of the eyelet. To finish, take the thread to the back through the centre hole on completion of the final stitch.

❶ *Left-handers work this stitch in mirror image.*

algerian eyelet stitch

Algerian eyelets are like regular counted eyelets, except that they have only three stitches per side instead of five. They are not as open as regular eyelets, so less tension is required.

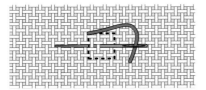

1 Using a tapestry needle, bring the thread out in the top left corner of a block of four by four threads. Insert the needle in the centre of the square. Bring it out two threads to the left.

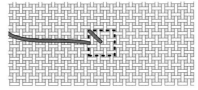

2 Pull the needle through, gently tightening the stitch a little.
❶ *Always insert the needle at the centre and bring it out at the edge.*

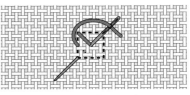

3 Insert the needle in the centre, bringing it in the bottom left corner of the square.

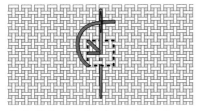

4 Pull the needle through, and gently tighten the stitch. Insert the needle in the centre, bringing it out two threads down.

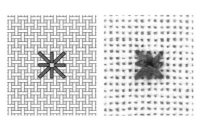

5 Continue working around the eyelet until it is complete.
❶ *Turn the work as needed, to assist with comfortable insertion of the needle.*

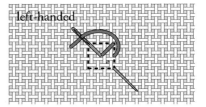

left-handed

❶ *Left-handers work this in mirror image, travelling clockwise.*

in a diagonal line

There are two stages: a journey to the end of the row down one side, then a journey back again on the other side.

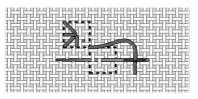

1 Work the first half of an eyelet (four stitches) then move on. Bring the needle out of the top left corner of the next eyelet. Insert it in the centre. Bring it out two threads left.
❶ *The eyelet corners are adjoining.*

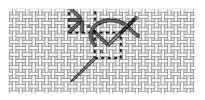

2 Continue working the first half of the eyelet, as before.

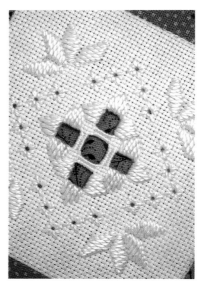

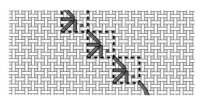

3 Work subsequent half eyelets.

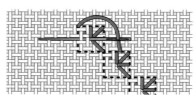

4 Turn the work 180 degrees. Continue around the end eyelet as before, to complete it.

5 Work subsequent half eyelets to complete the line.

feather stitch

Feather stitch is a versatile stitch with many variations. It is closely related to Cretan and buttonhole stitch. Also known as *single coral stitch*, and *briar stitch*. The unusual method which is shown here helps in creating very regular feather stitch.

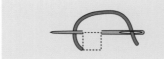

1 Use a small square as a guide. Bring the needle out in the square's bottom left corner. Insert the needle from the top right to the top left corner. Take the thread under the needle point.

2 Pull the needle through. With a new square immediately above the first, insert the needle from the top right to the top left corner. Take the thread under the needle point.

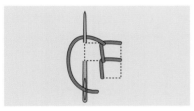

3 Pull the needle through. With a new square immediately to the left of the previous one, insert the needle from the bottom left to the top left corner. Take the thread under the needle point.

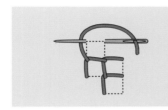

4 Pull the needle through. With a new square above the previous one, insert the needle from the top right to the top left corner. Take the thread under the needle point.

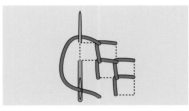

5 Pull the needle through. With a new square to the left of the previous one, insert the needle from the bottom left to the top left corner. Take the thread under the needle point.

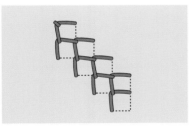

6 Continue in the same pattern. To finish, take a short stitch over the last stitch.

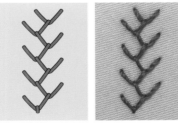

7 For the final effect, turn the work until the last stitch is at the bottom.

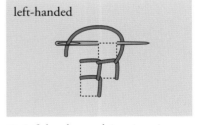

left-handed

❶ *Left-handers work in mirror image, travelling right and upwards.*

starting a new thread

1 Take the thread through to the back and leave the stitch a little loose on the front. Leave the end of the thread hanging on the back temporarily.

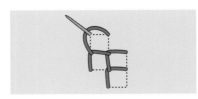

2 Fasten the new thread in the back of the existing stitching. Bring the new thread out ready to keep stitching.

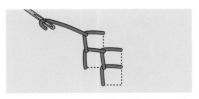

3 Pull the new thread through. Tighten the previous stitch to sit around it, as the others sit. Fasten the end of the old thread in the back of the stitching. Continue as before.

double feather stitch

Double feather stitch has two steps in each direction. It is also known as *double coral stitch*.

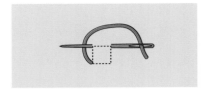

1 Use a small square as a guide. Bring the needle out in the square's bottom left corner. Insert the needle from the top right to the top left corner. Take the thread under the needle point.

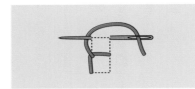

2 Pull the needle through. With a new square immediately above the first, insert the needle from the top right to the top left corner. Take the thread under the needle point.

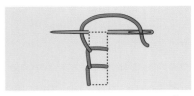

3 Pull the needle through. With a new square immediately above the previous one, insert the needle from the top right to the top left corner. Take the thread under the needle point.

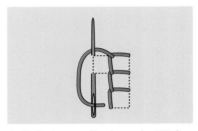

4 Pull the needle through. With a new square immediately to the left of the previous one, insert the needle from the bottom left to the top left corner. Take the thread under the needle point.

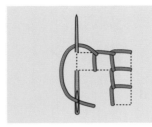

5 Pull the needle through. With a new square immediately to the left of the previous one, insert the needle from the bottom left to the top left corner. Take the thread under the needle point.

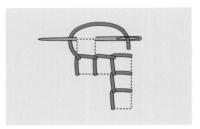

6 Pull the needle through. With a new square immediately above the previous one, insert the needle from the top right to the top left corner. Take the thread under the needle point.

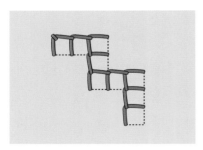

7 Continue in the same pattern. To finish, take a short stitch over the last stitch.

8 Turn the work until the last stitch is at the bottom.

left-handed

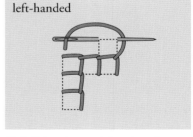

❶ *Left-handers work in mirror image, travelling right and upwards.*

❶ *By adjusting the spacing, different effects can be obtained.*

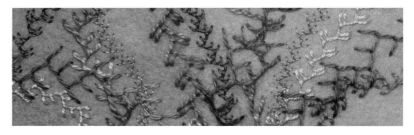

single feather stitch

This stitch is also known as *slanted buttonhole stitch*.

1 Use two guides. Bring the thread out on the left line. A little lower, insert the needle diagonally in the right line, exiting on the left. Loop the thread under the needle point.

2 Pull the needle through. Using the same angle and spacing, insert the needle from the right to the left line, with the needle point passing over the thread.

3 Repeat to build up a line of stitches. To finish, take a short stitch over the final feather stitch.

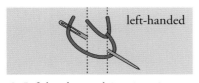

left-handed

❶ *Left-handers work in mirror image.*

long-armed feather stitch

This stitch is also known as *slanting Cretan stitch*.

 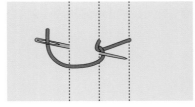

1 Use three guide lines. Bring the thread out on the middle line. Insert the needle on the right line, level with the emerging thread. Bring it out on the middle line, a little lower. Loop the thread under the needle point.

2 Pull the needle through. Using the same spacing and opposite angle, insert the needle in the left line, level with the emerging thread. Bring it out again a little lower on the middle line. Loop the thread under the needle point.

 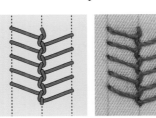 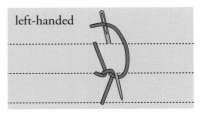

left-handed

3 Pull the needle through. Using the same spacing as before, insert the needle in the right line, bringing it on the middle line. Loop the thread under the needle point. Pull the needle through.

4 Continue working stitches on alternate sides of the middle line, finishing with a small straight stitch over the final feather stitch.

❶ *Left-handers work this stitch turned 90 degrees anticlockwise, travelling from left to right.*

closed feather stitch

Closed feather stitch is very similar to double chain stitch, but instead of the new stitches linking into the previous chains, they start from just below. Also similar to upright feather stitch, shown below.

1 Use two guides. Bring the thread out on the right line. Insert the needle in the left line and bring it out a short distance below so that the middle of the stitch is level with the emerging thread. Take the thread under the needle point.

2 Pull the needle through. Take a stitch in the right line, starting just below the previous stitch, using the same stitch length as before. Take the thread under the needle point.

 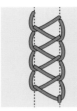

3 Pull the needle through. Take a stitch in the left line, starting just below the previous stitch, using the same stitch length as before. Take the thread under the needle point.

4 Continue in the same way to build up a line of stitching. Finish with a short stitch over the final stitch.
❶ *Left-handers work this stitch in exactly the same way.*

upright feather stitch

Upright feather stitch is also known as *coral stitch*. It is very similar to closed feather stitch.

1 Use two guides. Bring the thread out on the right line. Take a short stitch down the left line, just lower than the emerging thread. Loop the thread under the needle point.

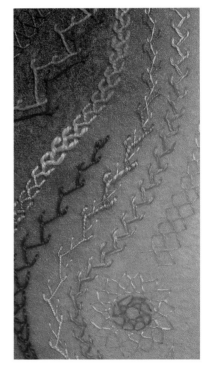

2 Pull the needle through. Take a stitch down the right line, using the same spacing and stitch length as before. Loop the thread under the needle point.

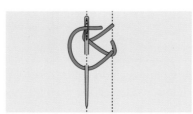

3 Pull the needle through. Make a stitch down the right line, using the same spacing and stitch length as before. Loop the thread under the needle point.

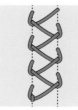 

4 Repeat steps 2 and 3 to build up a line of stitching. To finish, take a short stitch over the final stitch.
❶ *Left-handers work this stitch in exactly the same way.*

spanish knotted feather stitch

Also known as *twisted zigzag chain stitch*, this stitch works particularly well with heavier threads.

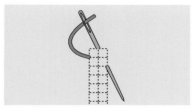

1 Use two columns of small squares as guides. Bring the thread out at the bottom left of the first square in the left column. Insert the needle in the top right corner of the same square. Bring it out in the top right corner of the third square in the right column.

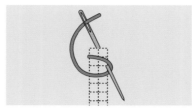

2 Take the thread to the right and then down behind the needle point, to the left.

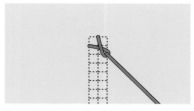

3 Pull the needle through, to create a twisted chain.

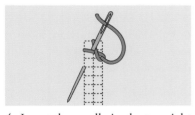

4 Insert the needle in the top right of the second square in the left column, just above the crossed threads of the twisted chain. Bring the needle out in the top left corner of the fourth square of the left column.

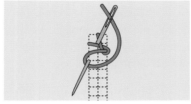

5 Take the thread left and then down behind the needle point, towards the right.

6 Pull the needle through.

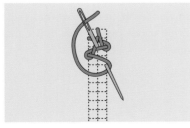 

7 Insert the needle in the top right of the third square of the left column, just above the crossed threads of the twisted chain. Bring the needle out in the top right of the fifth square of the right column. Take the thread right over and then down left behind the needle point.

8 Continue working twisted chains on alternating sides to build up a line of stitching.

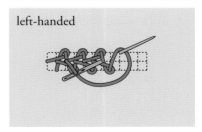

left-handed

❶ *Left-handers usually work this stitch rotated 90 degrees anticlockwise, travelling from left to right.*

florentine stitch

This stitch is known for its use in Florentine or bargello work. It has long stitches that are stepped up and down. Rows of different colours produce a pattern. Also known as *bargello stitch*, *cushion stitch*, *flame stitch*, *Hungary stitch* and *Irish stitch*. Use a tapestry needle.

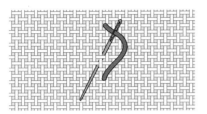

1 Bring the needle out. Insert it four threads up. Bring it out two threads down and one thread left.

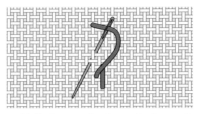

2 Pull the needle through. Insert it four threads up. Bring it out two threads down and one left.

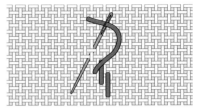

3 Pull the needle through. Insert it four threads up. Bring it out two threads down and one left.

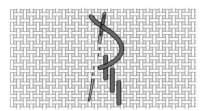

4 Pull the needle through. Insert it four threads up. Bring it out six threads down and one left.

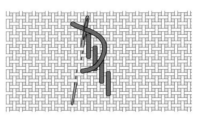

5 Pull the needle through. Insert it four threads up. Bring it out six threads down and one left.

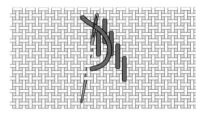

6 Pull the needle through. Insert it four threads up. Bring it out six threads down and one left.

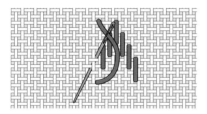

7 Pull the needle through. Insert it four threads up. Bring it out two threads down and one left.

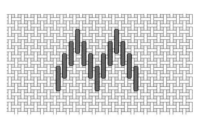

8 Continue stepping stitches up and down to build up a line of stitching.

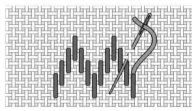

9 Using a new colour, bring the needle out at the top end of the first stitch. Insert it four threads up. Bring it out two threads down and one left.

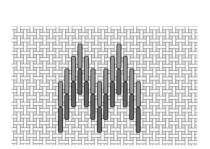

10 Continue with the new colour to build up a line of stitching.

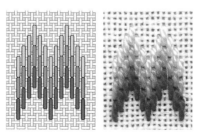

11 Work subsequent rows with new colours, in the same way.

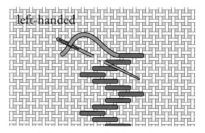

❶ *Left-handers work this stitch rotated 90 degrees anticlockwise.*

fly stitch

This stitch is also known as *'y' stitch*, *tied stitch* and *open loop stitch*. It is closely related to both chain and feather stitch. Fly stitch is usually anchored with a straight stitch, but variations can have chain stitch, or French or bullion knot anchor stitches.

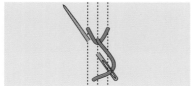

1 Use three lines. Bring the thread out on the left line. Level with it, insert the needle in the right line. Bring it out further down the centre line. Take the needle point over the thread.

2 Pull the needle through. A short distance below, insert the needle in the centre line. Using the same stitch length as in step 1, bring it out further up on the left line.

3 Pull the needle through. Insert the needle in the right line, level with the emerging thread, and bring it out at the bottom of the previous fly stitch on the centre line. Take the needle point over the thread.

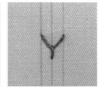
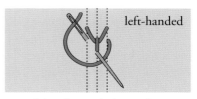

4 Continue to repeat steps 2 and 3 to build up a line of stitching. To finish, insert the needle in the centre line at the completion of a fly stitch.

❶ *For a single fly stitch, work step 1, and finish with a small stitch at the bottom.*

left-handed

❶ *Left-handers work this stitch in mirror image.*

tête de bœuf stitch

Tête de bœuf means bull's head in French, and is an apt name for this stitch because of its appearance. It is a variation of single fly stitch, anchored with a chain stitch instead of a straight stitch.

1 Use three guides. Bring the thread out on the left line. Level with that, insert the needle in the right line. Bring it out a little way down on the middle line. Take the thread under the needle point.

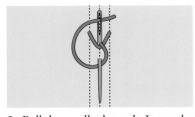

2 Pull the needle through. Insert the needle into the 'v' of the first stitch, where the thread emerges. Bring the needle out on the middle line a little below. Take the thread under the needle point.

3 Pull the needle through. Finish the chain stitch with a short anchoring stitch over its base.

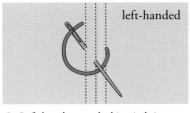

left-handed

❶ *Left-handers work this stitch in mirror image.*

italian knotted border stitch

This stitch is made up of a line of fly stitches which are anchored with French knots. It produces a very decorative border.

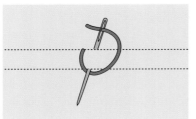

1 Use two guides. Bring the thread out on the top line. A little to the right, insert the needle in the top line. Bring it out halfway between the two points, on the bottom line. Take the thread under the needle point.

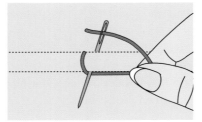

2 Take the right part of the loop in your right hand.

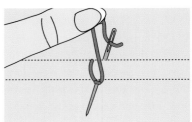

3 Wind it over the front of the needle point and up behind. Pull the thread up towards the top to make sure the wrap is snug around the needle.

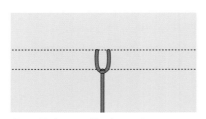

4 Pull the needle through.

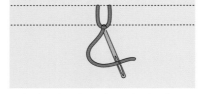

5 Take the thread to the back just below the knot.

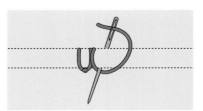

6 Bring the thread out just right of the first stitch. Using the same stitch length and spacing as before, take a stitch from the top to the bottom line. Take the thread under the needle point.

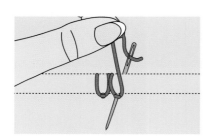

7 Wrap the thread around the needle point. Ensure the thread is snug around the needle, then pull the needle through.

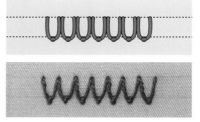

8 Continue making stitches to build up a line of stitches.

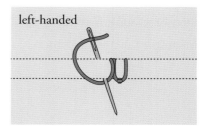

❶ *Left-handers work this stitch in mirror image.*

four-sided stitch

Four-sided stitch can be used as a pulled thread stitch, or worked with regular tension as a surface stitch. It is usually worked over a block of four by four threads. Also known as *square stitch*, or *four-sided openwork stitch*.

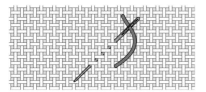

1 Using a tapestry needle, bring the thread out. Insert the needle four threads above, bringing it out four threads down and left.

❶ *To work it as a pulled thread stitch, gently tighten each stitch after it has been worked.*

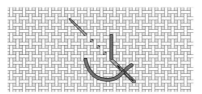

2 Pull the needle through. Insert it at the base of the previous stitch, bringing it out four threads up and left.

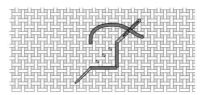

3 Pull the needle through. Insert it at the top of the upright stitch. Bring it out again in the opposite corner of the square.

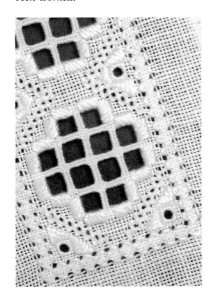

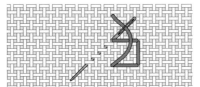

4 Pull the needle through. Insert the needle four threads up, and bring it out four threads down and left.

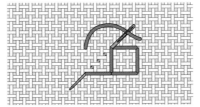

6 Pull the needle through. Insert it at the top of the last upright stitch. Bring it out again in the opposite corner of the square.

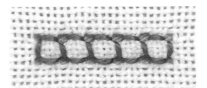

❶ *If each stitch is tightened, four-sided stitch can be used as a pulled thread stitch.*

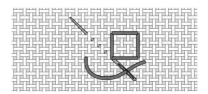

5 Pull the needle through. Insert the needle at the base of the last upright stitch. Bring it out four threads up and left.

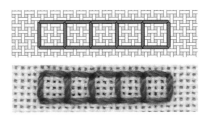

7 Continue in the same way to build up a line of stitching. Finish with an upright stitch at the end.

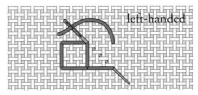

❶ *Left-handers work this stitch in mirror image.*

french knot

French knots are also known as *French dots, knotted stitch* and *twisted knot stitch.*

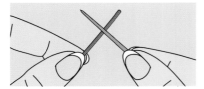 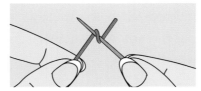 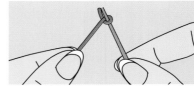

1 Use a milliner's needle. Bring the thread out of the fabric. Lay the needle on top of the thread.

2 Wind the thread around the needle once (or the number of times that are required). Take the needle point back over to where the thread emerges from the fabric.

❶ *More wraps will produce a larger knot.*

3 Insert the needle slightly to the right of the emerging thread (a few fabric threads in between).

❶ *Do not yet take the needle all the way through the fabric.*

❶ *If the needle goes in exactly the same hole, the knot may disappear to the back.*

 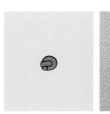 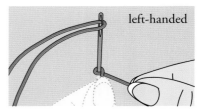

4 Hold the needle point below the fabric with your right hand. Tighten the wrap(s) at the base of the needle, so they sit flush against the fabric, to give a neat, compact knot.

5 Gently pull the needle and thread through to the back of the fabric to complete the finished knot.

❶ *Left-handers work this stitch in mirror image.*

pistil stitch

Also known as *long tack knot stitch, long-tailed French knot,* and *Italian knot stitch.* This stitch is a French knot with a long tail.

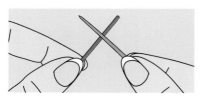 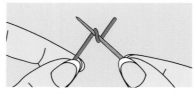 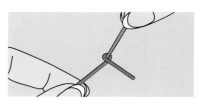

1 Use a milliner's needle. Bring the thread out of the fabric. Lay the needle on top of the thread.

2 Wind the thread around the needle once (or the number of times that are required).

❶ *More wraps create a larger knot.*

3 Insert the needle a little way away from where the thread emerges.

❶ *Do not yet take the needle all the way through the fabric.*

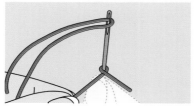  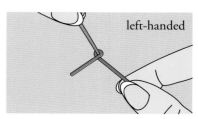

4 Holding the thread in your left hand, to maintain tension, pull the needle through from below.

5 Pull the needle and thread all the way through to create a small neat knot at the end of the stitch.

❶ *Left-handers work this stitch in mirror image.*

glove stitch

A decorative stitch for joining two pieces of fabric, or for edging a hem. It was historically used in the making of gloves.

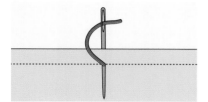

1 Use one guide line parallel to the edge of the fabric. Bring the needle out on the line. Insert the needle behind the fabric, bringing it out where the thread emerged.

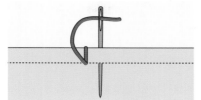

2 Pull the needle through. Moving to the right, insert the needle behind the fabric, bringing it out on the line.

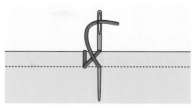

3 Pull the needle through. Insert the needle behind the fabric, bringing it out in the same place as the last stitch.

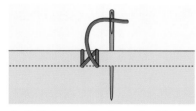

4 Pull the needle through. Moving to the right, insert the needle behind the fabric, bringing it out on the line.

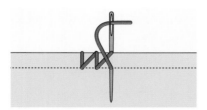

5 Pull the needle through. Insert the needle behind the fabric, bringing it out in the same place as before.

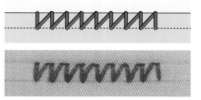

6 Continue in the same way to build up a line of stitching.
❶ *Left-handers work this stitch in exactly the same way.*

french glove stitch

French glove stitch is worked in mirror image to glove stitch.

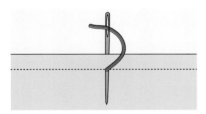

1 Use one guide line parallel to the edge of the fabric. Bring the needle out on the line. Insert the needle behind the fabric, bringing it out where the thread emerged.

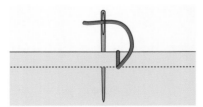

2 Pull the needle through. Moving to the left, insert the needle behind the fabric, bringing it out on the line.

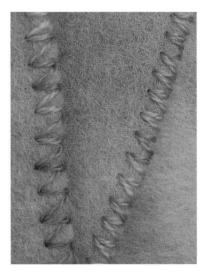

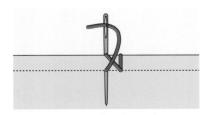

3 Pull the needle through. Insert the needle behind the fabric, bringing it out in the same place as the last stitch.

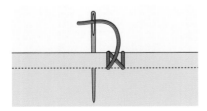

4 Pull the needle through. Moving to the left, insert the needle behind the fabric, bringing it out on the line.

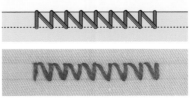

5 Continue in the same way to build up a line of stitching.
❶ *Left-handers work this stitch in exactly the same way.*

gobelin stitch

This stitch is also known as *oblique Gobelin stitch* and *slanted Gobelin stitch*. Use a tapestry needle.

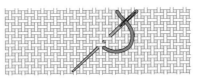

1 Bring the needle out. Insert it one thread right and two up. Bring it out again two threads down and left.

2 Pull the needle through. Insert it one thread right and two up. Bring it out again two threads down and left.

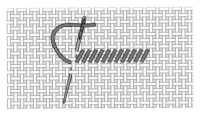

3 Continue stitching. To start the second row, insert the needle two threads up and one right. Bring it out four threads down and one left.

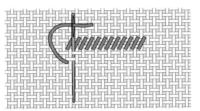

4 Pull the needle through. Insert it one thread right and two up. Bring it out again two threads down.

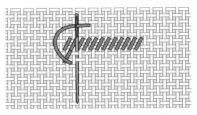

5 Continue inserting the needle one thread right and two up, and bringing it out two down. To start the next row, insert it two up and one right. Bring it out four down and one left.

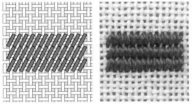

6 Continue alternating between the first and second rows.

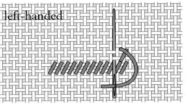

❶ *Left-handers work this turned 180 degrees.*

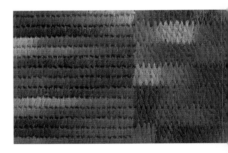

encroaching gobelin stitch

Also known as *interlocking Gobelin stitch* and *encroaching slanted Gobelin stitch*.

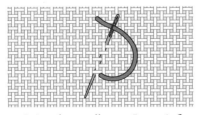

1 Bring the needle out. Insert it five threads up and one right. Bring it out five down and two left.

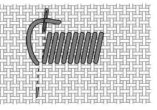

2 Continue in the same way. To start the new row, insert the needle five threads up and one right. Bring it out nine down and one left.

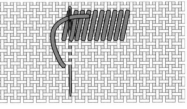

3 Pull the needle through. Insert it between the threads, five up and one right. Bring it out five threads below.

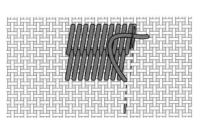

4 Continue in the same way. Start the new row by bringing out the needle nine threads down and one left.

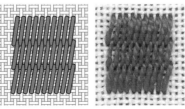

5 Continue across and back, taking each stitch one thread up into each previous row.

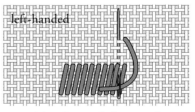

❶ *Left-handers work this turned 180 degrees.*

hedebo stitch

This is a firm edging stitch used in Danish hedebo embroidery. It can be worked close together or spaced apart.

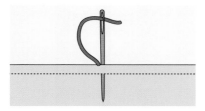

1 Use one guide. Bring the thread out at the folded fabric edge. Insert the needle at the back. Bring it out on the line right of the emerging thread.

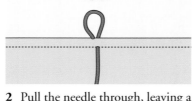

2 Pull the needle through, leaving a loop sitting up at the edge of the fabric.

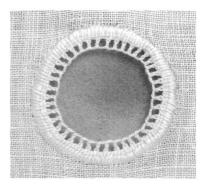

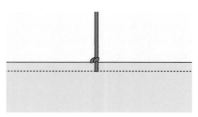

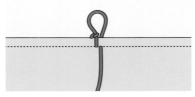

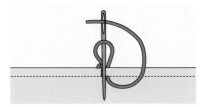

3 With the thread to the right, insert the needle in the back of the loop.

4 Pull the needle through and upwards.

5 Tighten so that the loop comes down to the edge of the fabric.

6 From the back, bring the needle out on the line right of the last stitch.

7 Pull the needle through, leaving a loop sitting up.

8 With the thread to the right, insert the needle into the back of the loop.

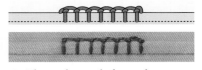

9 Pull the needle through and tighten so that the loop comes down to the edge of the fabric.

10 Continue similarly to build up a line of stitching. To finish, take the thread to the back at the edge.

❶ *The stitches worked spaced apart.*
❶ *Left-handers work this stitch in exactly the same way.*

working a second row

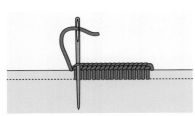

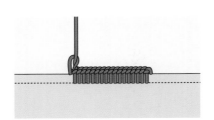

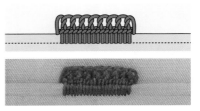

1 Work a base of closely spaced hedebo stitch. Bring the needle out at the edge. Insert it through the back of the top of the first stitch.

2 Make a stitch as shown above.
❶ *Because this is worked into a stitch not fabric, the result looks like twisted loops instead of buttonhole stitches.*

3 Work more stitches similarly, skipping a few base stitches each time to space the stitches apart. To finish, take the thread to the back at the edge.

hem stitch

Hem stitching is a beautiful way to edge a piece of embroidery as it has a neat and elegant finish. This method of hemstitching is worked from the front of the fabric, taking care to catch the hem fold into the stitching.

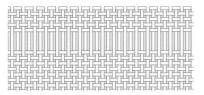

1 Remove two to three threads across the fabric to create a gap in which to work the decorative hem stitching.

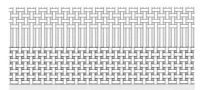

2 On the back of the fabric, create a hem, with the fold meeting the edge of the drawn thread area.

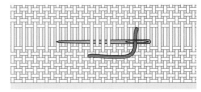

3 Turn the fabric over to the front. Bring a tapestry needle out two threads away from the gap, within the hem area. Count four threads right, and in the gap, slide the needle under four threads from right to left.
❶ *Any number of threads can be grouped, but three or four is usual.*

4 Pull the needle through, gently tightening, to pull the fabric threads together. Insert the needle in the gap right of the grouped threads. Bring the needle out two threads below, catching the hem fold into the stitch.
❶ *Ensure the needle goes through the folded hem as well.*

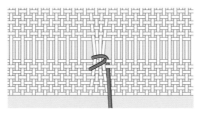

5 Pull the needle through and gently tighten the stitches.
❶ *Tightening the stitches pull the fabric threads together to create an openwork effect.*

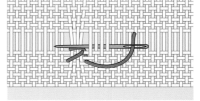

6 Count four threads right, and in the gap, slide the needle under four threads from right to left.

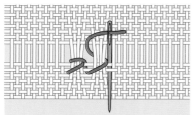

7 Pull the needle through, gently tightening, to pull the fabric threads together. Insert the needle in the gap right of the grouped threads. Bring the needle out two threads below, catching the hem fold into the stitch.
❶ *Ensure the needle goes through the folded hem as well.*

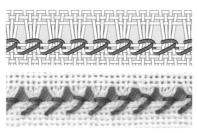

8 Continue in the same way to build up a line of stitching.

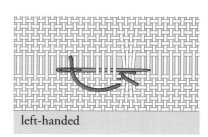

left-handed

❶ *Left-handers work this stitch in mirror image.*

antique hem stitch

This variation on regular hem stitch has a neater appearance on the front. It is worked from the back.

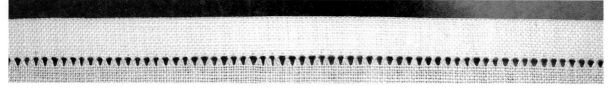

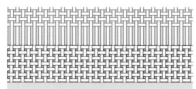 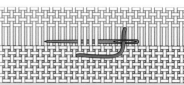

1 Remove two to three threads across the fabric to create a gap in which to work the decorative hem stitching.

2 On the back of the fabric, create a hem, with the fold meeting the edge of the drawn thread area.

3 Working on the back of the fabric, bring a tapestry needle out two threads away from the gap, within the hem area. Count four threads right, and in the gap, slide the needle under four threads from right to left.
❶ *Any number of threads can be grouped, but three or four is usual.*

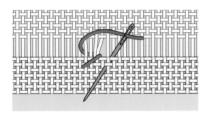 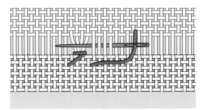 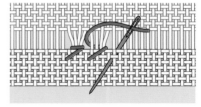

4 Pull the needle through, and gently tighten the stitch. Take the needle under the hem fold where it meets the drawn thread gap. Bring the needle out four threads right of where the thread first emerged.
❶ *The needle goes between the hem and the fabric front, only taking in the hem fabric, so that none of this stitch will be seen on the front.*

5 Pull the needle through and gently tighten the stitch to pull the threads together. Count four threads right, and in the gap, slide the needle under four threads from right to left.

6 Pull the needle through, and gently tighten the stitch. Take the needle under the hem fold, bringing it out four threads right of where the thread previously emerged from within the hem fold.

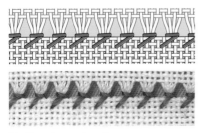 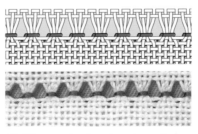 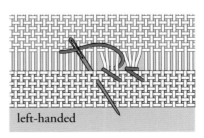

left-handed

7 Continue in the same way to build up a line of stitching.

❶ *The completed antique hem stitch as seen from the front of the fabric: only the grouping stitches show.*

❶ *Left-handers work this stitch in mirror image.*

herringbone stitch

Herringbone stitch can be worked with space between stitches (open), or with none (closed). Also known as *catch stitch, Mossoul stitch, Persian stitch, plaited stitch, Russian cross stitch, Russian stitch* and *witch stitch*.

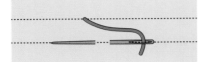

1 Use two guide lines. Bring the thread out on the top line. A little to the right, take a short stitch from right to left, on the bottom line. Pull the needle through.

2 Using the same spacing and stitch length as before, on the top line take a short stitch from right to left. Pull the needle through.

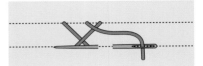

3 Using the same spacing and stitch length as before, take a short stitch in the bottom line, from right to left. Pull the needle through.

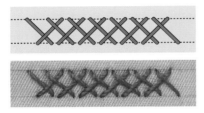

4 Repeat steps 2 and 3 to build up a line of stitching.

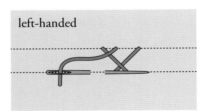

left-handed

❶ *Left-handers work herringbone stitch in mirror image, from right to left.*

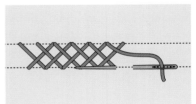

❶ *For closed herringbone, remove the gaps so that the stitches touch.*

threaded herringbone stitch

The threading can be in the same or a contrasting colour.

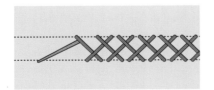

1 Work a foundation of herringbone stitch. Using a tapestry needle, bring a new thread out from under the far side of the stitch at the left end.

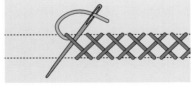

2 Without entering the fabric, slide the needle under the first stitch on the left, from above right.

3 Pull the needle through so that the thread wraps gently around the foundation. From below, slide the needle under the next stitch.

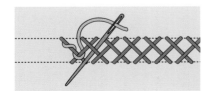

4 Pull the needle through so that the thread gently wraps the crossed stitches. Slide the needle in the opposite direction under the next stitch.

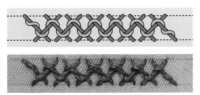

5 Continue in the same manner, sliding the needle under subsequent stitches from alternate sides. To finish take the thread to the back under the far side of the last stitch.

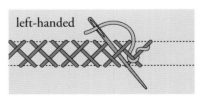

left-handed

❶ *Left-handers work this stitch in mirror image, from right to left.*

deerfield herringbone stitch

Also known as *tied herringbone stitch*, this stitch is used in Deerfield embroidery. Using a base of herringbone stitch, each pair of crossed threads is couched in place.

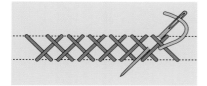

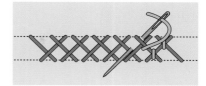

1 Work a foundation of herringbone stitch. Bring the needle out below the right-most cross. Insert the needle above the cross, bringing it out again just above the next cross.

2 Pull the needle through. Insert the needle on the far side of the cross. Bring the needle out again on the near side of the next cross.

3 Pull the needle through. Insert the needle on the far side of the cross. Bring the needle out again on the near side of the next cross.

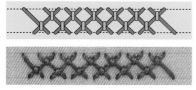

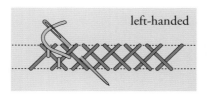

4 Continue stitching, couching each pair of crossed threads.

❶ *Left-handers work from left to right.*

herringbone ladder filling stitch

Also known as *interlaced band* or *laced Cretan stitch*. Use a foundation of two lines of running, back or Holbein stitch, where the centres of the stitches in one line align with the ends of the stitches in the other. Use a tapestry needle.

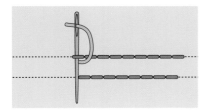

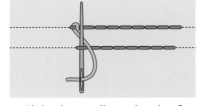

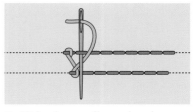

1 Bring the thread out just below the left-most stitch. Slide the needle under the stitch from above, with the thread under the needle point.
❶ *Do not enter the fabric at any point.*

2 Slide the needle under the first stitch in the opposite line, from below. Take the thread under the needle point.
❶ *The needle always points to the centre.*

3 Slide the needle under the next stitch in the opposite line, from above. Take the thread under the needle point.

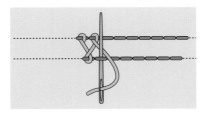

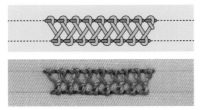

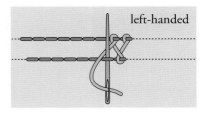

4 Slide the needle under the first stitch in the opposite line, from below. Take the thread under the needle point.

5 Continue in the same way to fill the foundation stitches with ladder filling. To finish, take a short stitch over the last lacing.

❶ *Left-handers work from right to left.*

double herringbone stitch – method one

Double herringbone stitch is often best worked in two colours, for the contrast produced. There are two methods for working this stitch.

1 Use two guides, and work a line of well-spaced herringbone stitch.

2 Bring a new coloured thread out at the left end of the stitching, on the lower line. Take a stitch from right to left in the top line, opposite the first cross of the first colour. Use the same stitch length as before.

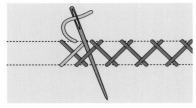

3 Pull the needle through. Slide the needle from above, under the second stitch.
❶ *Do not enter the fabric.*

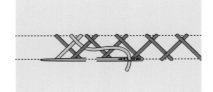

4 Take a stitch from right to left, in the lower line, between the second and third stitches of the first colour, using similar spacing as previously.

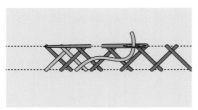

5 Pull the needle through. Take a stitch from right to left in the top line, between the next two stitches of the first colour.

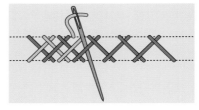

6 Pull the needle through. Slide the needle from above, under the next stitch of the first colour.
❶ *Do not enter the fabric.*

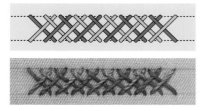

7 Continue in the same manner to fill in the spaces between the first colour's stitches.

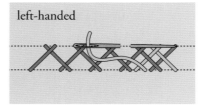

left-handed

❶ *Left-handers work this stitch in mirror image, travelling from right to left.*

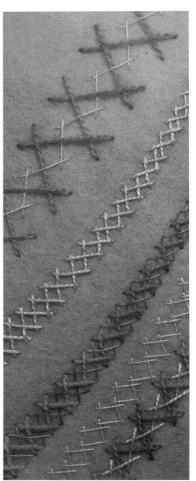

double herringbone stitch – method two

This is the more complicated of the two methods, and is necessary as the foundation for working interlaced herringbone stitch.

1 Use two guides. Bring the needle out on the bottom line. On the top line, a little to the right, take a short stitch from right to left. Take the thread under the needle point.

2 Pull the needle through. Using the same spacing and stitch length as before, take a stitch in the bottom line, from right to left.
❶ *The threads cross with the working thread under the first stitch.*

3 Pull the needle through. Take another stitch in the top line, with the thread under the needle point.
❶ *The threads cross with the working thread over the previous stitch.*

4 Continue in the same manner to build up a line of stitching.

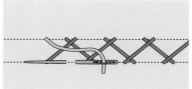

5 Bring a new thread out at the left end of the stitching, on the top line. Take a stitch in the bottom line, opposite the first cross.

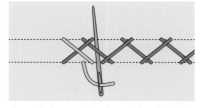

6 Pull the needle through. Slide the needle under the next stitch, from below.
❶ *Do not enter the fabric.*

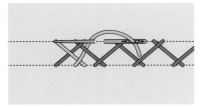

7 Take another stitch in the top line, with the thread under the needle point.

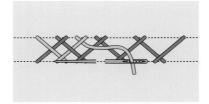

8 Pull the needle through. Take a stitch in the bottom line.
❶ *Note how the middle crosses all go the same way, and the outer crosses all cross the opposite way.*

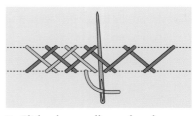

9 Slide the needle under the next stitch from below.
❶ *Do not enter the fabric.*

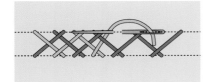

10 Take a stitch in the top line, with the thread under the needle point.

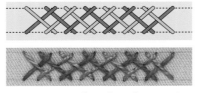

11 Keeping the threads crossing correctly, continue in the same manner to build up a line of stitches.

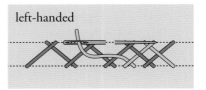

❶ *Left-handers work this stitch rotated 180 degrees.*

left-handed

103

interlaced herringbone stitch

This is a complicated stitch, but with practise a rhythm will form.

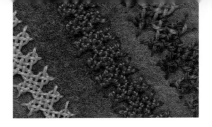

1 Begin with a foundation of double herringbone stitch – method 2.
❶ *If any of the stitches cross the wrong way, the interlacing will not work.*
❶ *Note the shortened end stitches.*

2 Using a tapestry needle, bring the thread out just above the right-most cross. Moving down and left, skip the first thread, and slide the needle under the next thread.
❶ *Do not enter the fabric at any time.*

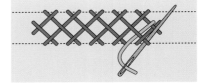

3 Moving around the cross in an anticlockwise direction, skip the adjacent spoke and slide the needle under the next one, from above.

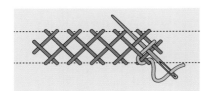

4 Moving up and left, skip the foundation thread, and slide the needle under both the lacing thread and the next foundation thread.

5 Turn the needle to work down and left. Skip the first foundation thread, and slide the needle under the next one.

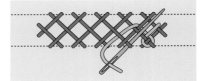

6 Moving around the cross in an anticlockwise direction, skip the first spoke and slide the needle under the next one, from below.

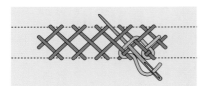

7 Pass the foundation thread, and slide the needle under the lacing and the next foundation thread.

8 Continue lacing to the end of the row.

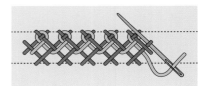

9 Turn the work 180 degrees. Going round the end cross, miss a spoke and slide the needle under the next one.

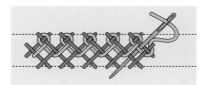

10 Moving down and left, miss the first thread, and pass under the second and third.

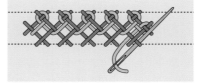

11 Moving around the cross, miss a spoke and slide the needle under the next one.

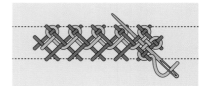

12 Moving up and left, pass the needle over, then under, over, then under the threads.

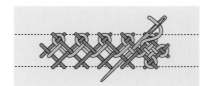

13 Moving down and left, miss the first thread, and pass under the second and third.

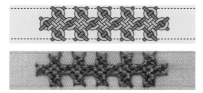

14 Continue lacing the foundation stitches. Take the thread to the back where it meets the beginning.

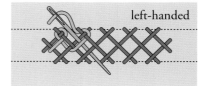

left-handed

❶ *Left-handers work this stitch turned 180 degrees, working right along the top, then along the bottom.*

hollie stitch

This stitch is used in Hollie point lace. Also known as *Holy point* and *Holy stitch*.

1 Outline the shape in short chain stitches. Change to a tapestry needle. Bring the thread out in the top chain on the right side.

2 Take the thread to the back in the top chain on the left side to create a laid stitch.

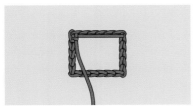

3 Bring the thread out at the bottom of the same chain. Place the needle under the left-most chain at the top, and the laid stitch. Take the thread under the needle point.

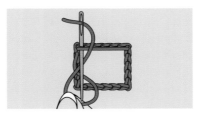

4 Take the thread coming from the eye under the needle point, over the working thread, from right to left.
❶ *This creates a crossed loop under the needle point.*

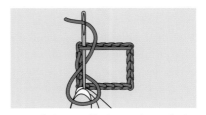

5 Pull the needle down through the loop.

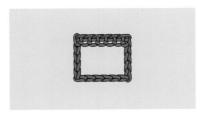

6 The completed hollie stitch.

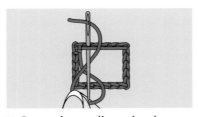

7 Insert the needle under the next chain along and the laid thread. Make another crossed loop as before.

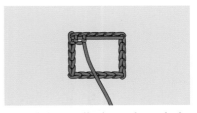

8 Pull the needle down through the loop and tighten to create another hollie stitch.

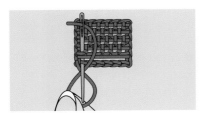

9 Work across to the far side of the shape working a stitch into each chain and under the laid stitch. Take the thread to the back in the chain.

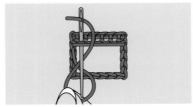

10 Work a laid stitch from right to left. Bring the needle out in the next chain and work a stitch into each loop and under the laid stitch.

11 Work the rest of the row in the same way. Continue filling the shape by working laid stitches and rows of hollie stitches.

12 Work the last row with each stitch taking in the previous row's loop, the laid stitch and the bottom chain stitch row.

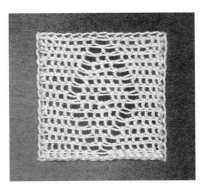

13 The completed hollie point.
❶ *Left-handers work this stitch in exactly the same way.*

jessica stitch

This stitch uses a series of straight stitches to create arcs or full circles. Jessica stitches can be any size and adapted to many shapes.

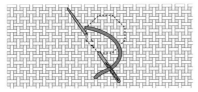

1 Bring a tapestry needle out on the edge of the shape. Count four holes along the edge in an anticlockwise direction and insert the needle. Bring it out one hole along from where the thread last emerged.

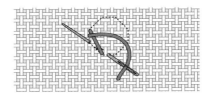

2 Pull the needle through. Count four holes along the edge and insert the needle. Bring it out one hole along from where the thread last emerged.

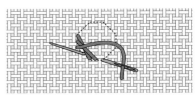

3 Continue in the same way around the edge of the shape until your stitch meets the first stitch.

❶ *Turn the work as necessary to assist with inserting the needle.*

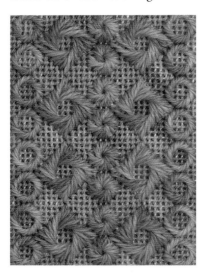

❶ *When you have gone nearly the whole way around the edge of the shape, the stitches will meet. If you keep stitching in the same way, the last stitches will sit on top of the first few stitches. However, the aim is to slip the last ones in under the first few, so that the overlap is seamless.*

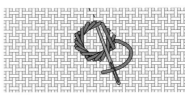

4 Turn the shape so that the first few stitches are at the top. Insert the needle under the stitches into the next hole.

5 Pull the needle through. Bring the needle out in the next hole along from where it last emerged. Insert it under the first few stitches and into the next hole along from where you last emerged.

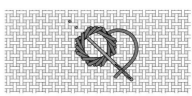

6 Pull the needle through. Bring the needle out in the next hole along from where it last emerged. Insert it under the first few stitches and into the next hole along from where you last emerged.

7 The completed stitch.

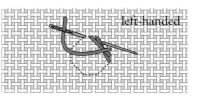

left-handed

❶ *Left-handers work the stitch rotated 180 degrees.*

❶ *Longer stitches (shown above) will create a smaller central hole. Shorter stitches create a larger centre hole.*

long and short stitch

Long and short stitch is also known as *brick stitch, embroidery stitch, feather work, Irish stitch, leaf stitch, opus plumarium, plumage stitch, shading stitch,* and *tapestry shading stitch.*

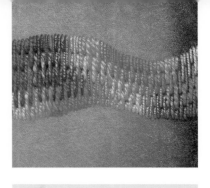

1 Use a series of parallel lines. Bring the thread out on the third line. Directly above, insert the needle in the top line, bringing it out just to the left on the second line.

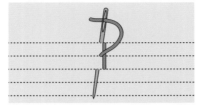

2 Pull the needle through. In the top line, insert the needle directly above where the thread emerges. Bring the needle out slightly to the left on the third line.

3 Pull the needle through. In the top line, insert the needle directly above where the thread emerges. Bring the needle out slightly to the left on the second line.

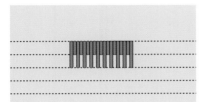

4 Continue similarly to build up a line of alternating length stitches.
❶ *The stitch tops align, but there is a stitch space between the stitches at the bottom.*

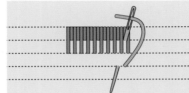

5 Bring a new colour out on the fourth line, aligning with the space between the first and third stitches. Take a stitch from the second line to the fourth line, emerging between the third and fifth stitches.

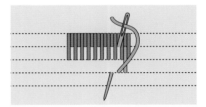

6 Pull the needle through. Take a stitch from the fourth to the second lines, to fill the space between the next two stitches.
❶ *There is a stitch space between each of the stitches.*

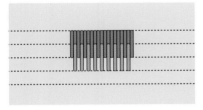

7 Continue in the same way to fill the line.

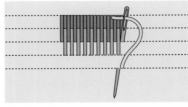

8 Bring a new colour out at the beginning of the fifth line. Insert the needle directly above, in the second line, bringing it out next to the emerging thread on the fifth line.

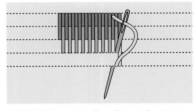

9 Pull the needle through. Insert the needle directly above on the fourth line. Bring the needle out next to the emerging thread on the fifth line.

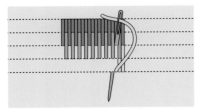

10 Pull the needle through. Take another stitch to fill the next gap.

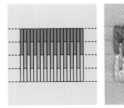

11 Continue in the same way to complete the line.

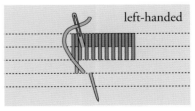

left-handed

❶ *Left-handers work this stitch in mirror image.*

irregular long and short stitch

This stitch is used for *needle painting*, *silk shading* and *thread painting*. Careful blending of rows creates a smooth change between colours. Practise is required to master this stitch.

1 Use a single fine thread. Outline the petal shape in split stitch.
❶ *The finer the thread, the more delicate the colour shading can be.*

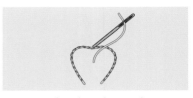

2 Bring the thread out about one third the way down the petal, in the centre. Insert the needle just under the outline stitching from above.
❶ *This will help to conceal the end of the stitch to create a smooth edge.*

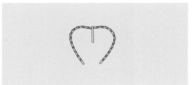

3 Pull the needle through.

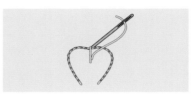

4 Bring the thread out right next to the beginning of the previous stitch, but a little higher. Insert the needle over the far side of the split stitch.
❶ *Work the stitches very close together, but not on top of one another, to create a good foundation for the next row.*

5 Pull the thread through. Continue working out to one side, with the start of each stitch alternately longer or shorter than the previous one.
❶ *Fan the stitches as needed to fit with the curve.*

6 From the centre, work out to the other side, alternating the length of the stitches.
❶ *No two adjacent stitches should be of the same length.*

7 With a new colour, bring the needle out through the centre stitch of the first row, about half to one third the way back from the stitch end.
❶ *Always come up in the previous row's stitches, and go down into the fabric.*

8 Insert the needle further down the petal, following the direction of the stitch it overlaps.
❶ *Longer overlaps with the previous row enable better colour blending.*

9 Pull the needle through. Work the rest of the row out to one side, and then the other. Stagger the start and finish of each stitch, and follow the direction of the stitches they overlap.

10 Work the next row in the same way as before, in a new colour.
❶ *Ensure that no fabric is showing through between the stitches.*

11 Work the final row, with the bottoms of the stitches roughly aligning.
❶ *Left-handers work this stitch similarly, angling their needle from the left.*

loop stitch

This stitch is also known as *centipede stitch* or *knotted loop stitch*.

1 Use two guide lines. Bring the thread out centred between the two lines. A short distance to the left, vertically insert the needle from the top to the bottom line.

2 Pull the needle through. From above right, slide the needle under the first stitch and over the working thread.
❶ *Do not enter the fabric.*

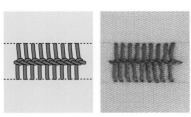

3 Pull the needle through to create a gentle loop around the previous stitch. Using the same spacing across as before, take a vertical stitch from the top line to the bottom line.

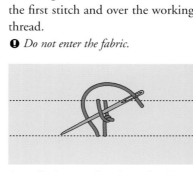

4 Pull the needle through. From above right, slide the needle under the previous stitch, and over the working thread.
❶ *Do not enter the fabric.*

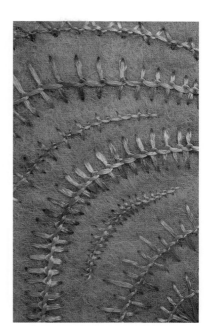

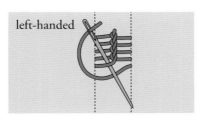

5 Continue in the same manner to build up a line of stitching. To finish, take the thread to the back just left of the final loop.

left-handed

❶ *Left-handers work this stitch turned 90 degrees anticlockwise, travelling from top to bottom.*

montenegrin stitch

This stitch is also known as *two-sided Montenegrin cross stitch* and *Montenegrin cross stitch*.

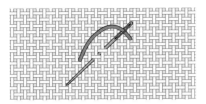

1 Bring a tapestry needle out. Insert it four threads right and two up. Bring it out two threads down and left.

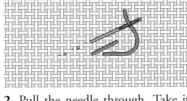

2 Pull the needle through. Take it to the back two threads up and left.

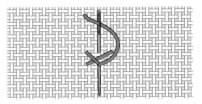

3 Bring the needle out two threads down and right. Insert it up two. Bring it out where the thread emerged.

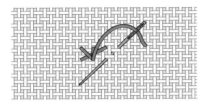

4 Pull the needle through. Insert it four threads right and two up. Bring it out two threads down and left.

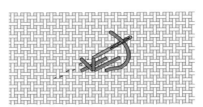

5 Pull the needle through. Take it to the back two threads up and left.

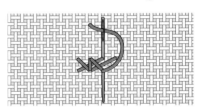

6 Bring the needle out two threads down and right. Insert it up two. Bring it out where the thread emerged.

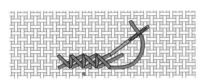

7 Continue stitching in the same way. To begin to finish, complete the vertical stitch.

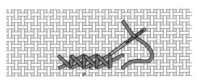

8 Bring the needle out two threads down and right. Take the thread to the back two threads up and left.

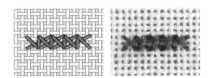

9 The finished Montenegrin stitch.

turning corners

left-handed

❶ *Left-handers work this stitch turned 90 degrees anticlockwise.*

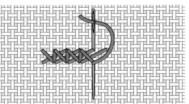

1 To make a right hand turn, work through the sequence, last making a vertical stitch.

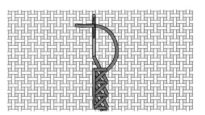

2 Turn the work 90 degrees anticlockwise. Pull the needle through. Insert it two threads left and up. Bring it out two threads down.

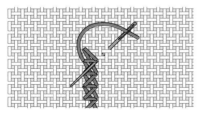

3 Pull the needle through. Insert it four threads right and two up. Bring it out two threads down and left.

4 Pull the needle through. Insert it two threads up and bring it out two threads down.

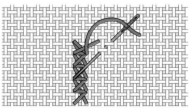

5 Pull the needle through. Insert it four threads right and two up. Bring it out two down and left.

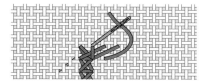

6 Pull the needle through. Cycle through the steps as before to continue in the new direction.

7 To make a left hand turn, work through the sequence, complete the vertical stitch, and bring the needle out two threads down and right.

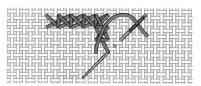

8 Turn the work 90 degrees clockwise. Pull the needle through. Insert it four threads right and two up. Bring it out two down and left.

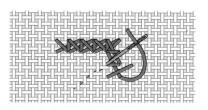

9 Pull the needle through. Take the needle to the back two threads up and left.

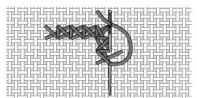

10 Bring the needle out two threads down and right. Insert it two threads up and bring it out where the thread emerged.

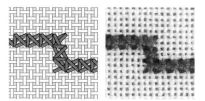

11 Continue stitching as before.

diagonal montenegrin stitch

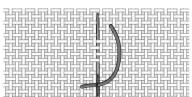

1 Bring the needle out. Insert it six threads down and two left. Bring it out four threads up.

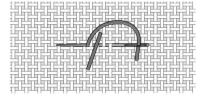

2 Pull the needle through. Insert it four threads right, bringing it out where the thread emerged.

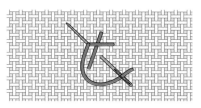

3 Pull the needle through. Insert it two threads down and right. Bring it out where the thread emerged.

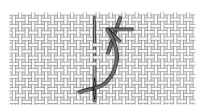

4 Pull the needle through. Insert it six threads down and two left. Bring it out four threads up.

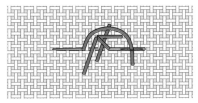

5 Pull the needle through. Insert it four threads right, bringing it out where the thread emerged.

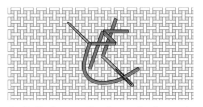

6 Pull the needle through. Insert it two threads down and right. Bring it out where the thread emerged.

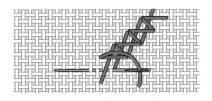

7 Continue stitching in the same way. To begin to finish, complete the short diagonal stitch, and bring the needle out four threads to the left.

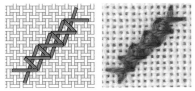

8 Pull the needle through. Take the thread to the back four threads to the right to complete the diagonal Montenegrin stitch.

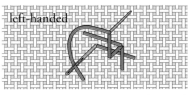

❶ *Left-handers work this stitch turned 90 degrees clockwise.*

mountmellick stitch

This linear stitch comes from Irish Mountmellick embroidery.

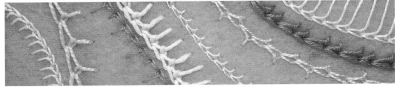

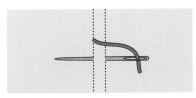

1 Use two guide lines. Bring the thread out on the left line. A little way down, horizontally insert the needle from the right to the left line.

2 Pull the needle through. From above right, slide the needle under the diagonal stitch, keeping the working thread out of the way.
❶ *Do not enter the fabric.*

3 Gently pull the thread down so that it fits snugly around the first stitch.

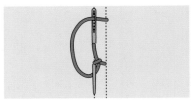

4 On the left line, take a stitch from the top of the first stitch to the left end of the second stitch. Take the thread under the needle point.
❶ *This will create a chained stitch.*

5 Pull the needle through.

6 Using the same stitch spacing as before, horizontally insert the needle from the right to the left line.

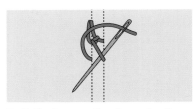

7 Pull the needle through. From above right, slide the needle under the diagonal stitch. Keep the working thread out of the way.
❶ *Do not enter the fabric.*

8 Gently pull the thread down so that it fits snugly around the first stitch.

9 Insert the needle in the previous chained stitch, bringing it out at the bottom of the last stitch. Take the thread under the needle point.

10 Pull the needle through.

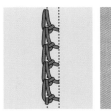

11 Continue in the same manner to build up a line of stitching. To finish, take a short stitch over the final chained stitch.

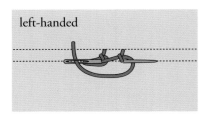

left-handed

❶ *Left-handers work this stitch turned 90 degrees anticlockwise, travelling from left to right.*

112

mountmellick thorn stitch

Thorn stitch is unique to Mountmellick embroidery and is a feather stitch incorporating a French knot.

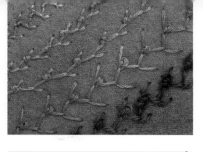

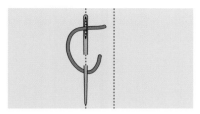

1 Use two guides. Bring the thread out between the lines. Level with that, take a stitch in the left line, with the thread below the needle point.

2 Pull the needle through. Using the same stitch length as previously, take a stitch in the right line slightly lower than before. Take the thread under the needle point.

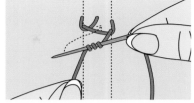

3 Pull the needle through. Wrap the thread under and around the needle three times. Take the needle point up and over the bottom of the previous stitch.

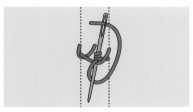

4 Insert the needle under the previous stitch and a few fabric threads underneath. Tighten the wraps round the needle. Take the thread across then right under the needle point.

5 Pull the needle through to complete the French knot.

6 Level with the emerging thread, take a stitch in the left line, with the thread below the needle point.

7 Pull the needle through. Using the same stitch length as previously, take a stitch in the right line slightly lower than before. Take the thread under the needle point.

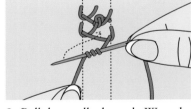

8 Pull the needle through. Wrap the thread under and around the needle three times. Take the needle point up and over the bottom of the previous stitch.

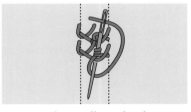

9 Insert the needle under the previous stitch and a few fabric threads underneath. Tighten the knot wraps around the needle. Take the thread under the needle point.

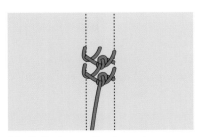

10 Pull the needle through.

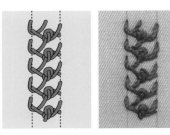

11 Continue in the same way to build up a line of stitching. To finish, take the thread to the back at the base of the French knot.

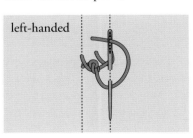

left-handed

❶ *Left-handers work this stitch in mirror image.*

needlewoven bars

Needlewoven or *needleweaving bars* are a drawn thread stitch, often used as a decoration in hemstitching and in Hardanger embroidery. Threads are withdrawn from the fabric, then the remaining threads are decoratively woven back together.

1 Remove some threads down the fabric to create a gap in which to work the woven bars.

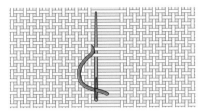

2 Using a tapestry needle, bring the thread out at the left edge of the drawn thread area, in the middle of the four threads that will form the bar. From below, slide the needle under the two threads below the emerging thread.

❶ *Four threads are woven together here, but any number can be used.*

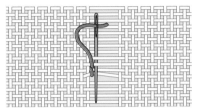

3 Pull the needle through and gently tighten the stitch to pull the threads together. From above, slide the needle under the two threads above the emerging thread.

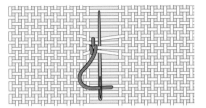

4 Pull the needle through and gently tighten the stitch to pull the threads together. From below, slide the needle under the two threads below the emerging thread.

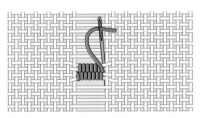

5 Keep working stitches on alternate sides of the bar to fill the space. Finish with a stitch on the opposite side to the one you started on, and take the thread to the back.

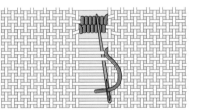

6 To work the next bar, bring the thread out at the right side of the drawn thread area, two threads below the first bar. From below, slide the needle under the two threads below the emerging thread.

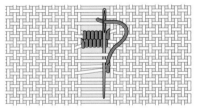

7 Pull the needle through and gently tighten the stitch to pull the threads together. From above, slide the needle under the two threads above the emerging thread.

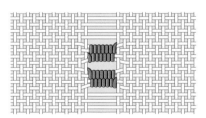

8 Work stitches on alternate sides of the bar to fill the space. Finish with a stitch on the opposite side to the one you started on, and take the thread to the back.

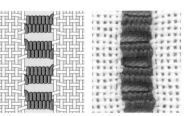

9 Continue working bars back and forth, to fill the drawn thread area as required.

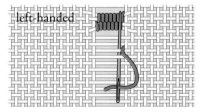

❶ *Left-handers work this stitch similarly, but angle their needle in a more left-handed way.*

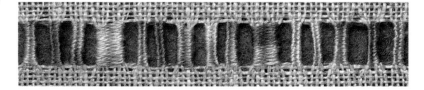

norwich stitch

Also known as *waffle stitch*, this stitch must always span an odd number of threads.

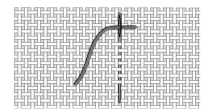

1 Bring a tapestry needle out. Insert it seven threads up and right. Bring it out seven threads below.

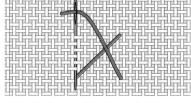

2 Pull the needle through. Insert it seven threads up and left, bringing it out six threads below.

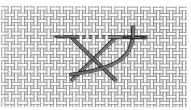

3 Pull the needle through. Take the thread to the back six threads up and right.

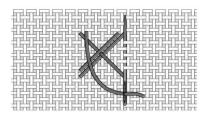

4 Bring the needle out five threads left. Insert it six threads down and right. Bring it out five threads above.

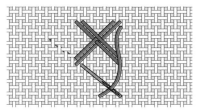

5 Pull the needle through. Insert it six threads left and down.

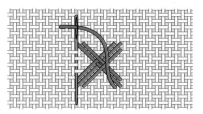

6 Bring the needle out five threads right. Insert it six threads up and left. Bring it out four threads below.

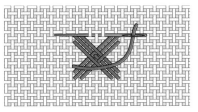

7 Pull the needle through. Take it to the back five threads up and right.

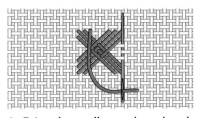

8 Bring the needle out three threads left. Insert the needle five threads down and right. Bring it out three above.

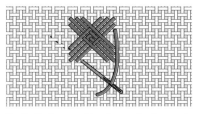

9 Pull the needle through. Insert it five threads down and left.

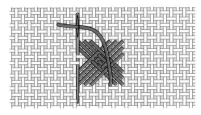

10 Bring the needle out three threads right. Insert it five threads up and left. Bring it out two threads below.

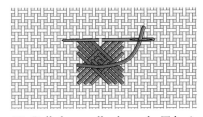

11 Pull the needle through. Take it to the back four threads up and right.

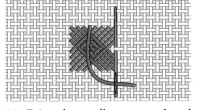

12 Bring the needle out one thread left. Insert it four threads down and right. Bring it out one thread above.

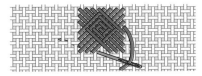

13 Pull the needle through. Insert it four threads down and left.

14 Bring the needle out one thread to the right. Take it to the back in the left side in the only remaining space.

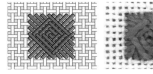

15 The completed stitch.
❶ *Left-handers work this in exactly the same sequence.*

nun stitch

This stitch is used as a border stitch and also as an edging. Each stitch is worked twice. It can be worked with regular tension or pulled tight for more stability, especially when used as an edging.

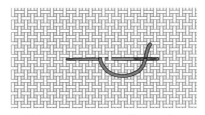

1 Bring a tapestry needle out. Insert it two threads to the right, bringing it out in the same hole as where the thread first emerged.

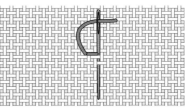

2 Pull the needle through. Insert the needle two threads to the right. Bring it out two threads below.

❶ *For an edge stitch, gently tighten each stitch, making it more firm and stable.*

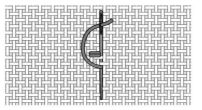

3 Pull the needle through. Insert it two threads above, bringing it out where the thread last emerged.

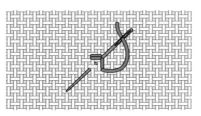

4 Pull the needle through. Insert the needle two threads above. Bring it out two threads down and left.

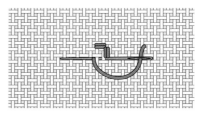

5 Pull the needle through. Insert it two threads to the right, bringing it out where the thread last emerged.

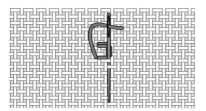

6 Pull the needle through. Insert it two threads to the right. Bring the needle out two threads below.

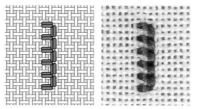

7 Continue in the same way to build up a line of stitching.

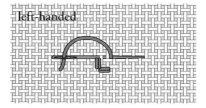

left-handed

❶ *Left-handers work this stitch turned 180 degrees, from bottom to top.*

turning a corner

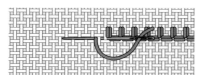

1 Work up to the corner, finishing with step 6 (above). Turn the work 90 degrees clockwise. Pull the needle through. Insert it two threads to the right. Bring it out two threads left.

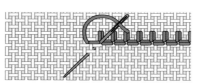

2 Pull the needle through. Insert the needle two threads to the right. Bring it out two threads down and left.

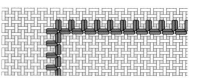

3 Continue stitching as before.

edging with nun stitch

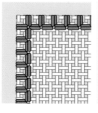

When working as an edging, after each stitch, gently tighten the thread, to make the stitching more firm and sturdy. On completion, cut away to the edge of the stitching, taking care not to cut any stitches.

❶ *Extreme care should be taken when using this stitch as an edging. If the fabric is cut away from the edge, it is very easy to accidentally pull the whole edging away. If this is of concern, use a different edging stitch.*

palestrina stitch

Also known as *double knot stitch, old English knot stitch, Palestrina knot stitch, Smyrna stitch* and *tied coral stitch.*

1 Use one guide. Bring the thread out on the line. A short way below, take a short stitch from right to left, from one side of the line to the other.

2 Pull the needle through. Slide the needle under the stitch from right to left.
❶ *Do not enter the fabric.*

3 Pull the thread through so that it fits snugly around the first stitch, without pulling the first stitch out of shape.

4 From above right, slide the needle under the lower section of the first stitch. Take the needle over the thread.
❶ *Do not enter the fabric.*

5 Pull the needle through. Using the same stitch spacing as before, take a short stitch from right to left, from one side of the line to the other.

6 Repeat steps 2 to 5 as needed. To finish, take a short stitch into the fabric at the end of step 4.

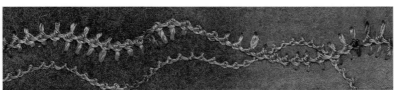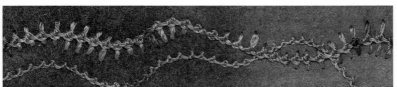

left-handed

❶ *Left-handers work this stitch turned 180 degrees, from bottom to top.*

long-armed palestrina stitch

Long-armed Palestrina stitch is worked similarly to regular Palestrina stitch, but the first stitch of each knot is much longer, making it look more like a ribbed spine.

1 Use two guides. Bring the thread out between them. A short way below, take a horizontal stitch from the right to the left line.

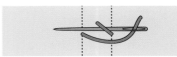

2 Pull the needle through. Slide the needle from right to left under the stitch.
❶ *Do not enter the fabric.*

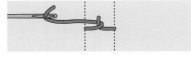

3 Pull the needle through so that the thread fits snugly around the first stitch.

4 From above, slide the needle under the right section of the first stitch. Take the needle over the working thread.
❶ *Do not enter the fabric.*

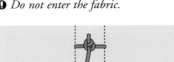

5 Gently pull the thread through to tighten it into a small neat knot.

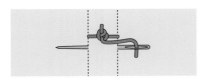

6 Using the same spacing as before, take a horizontal stitch from the right line to the left line.

7 Repeat steps 2 to 6 as needed. To finish, take a short stitch into the fabric at the end of step 5.

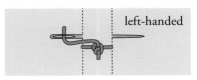

left-handed

❶ *Left-handers work this stitch turned 180 degrees, from bottom to top.*

sorbello stitch

This stitch is like Palestrina stitch but in reverse. It can be used individually in much the same way as cross stitch to build up designs.

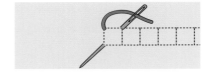

1 Use squares as guides. Bring the thread out in the top left-most corner. Insert the needle from the top right to the bottom left of the square.

2 Pull the needle through. From above right, slide the needle under the straight stitch.
❶ *Do not enter the fabric.*

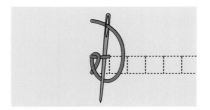

3 Pull the needle through and leave the stitch hanging loosely. From above right, slide the needle under the right part of the straight stitch and over the working thread.

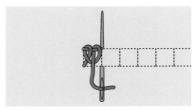

4 Pull the needle through. Leave the stitch hanging down. Insert the needle from the bottom to the top right of the square.
❶ *Take the thread to the back for a single sorbello stitch.*

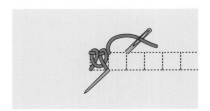

5 To begin working the next sorbello stitch, insert the needle in the top right corner of the next square and bring it out in the bottom left corner.

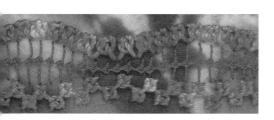

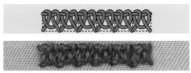

6 Continue working through the steps to build up a line of stitching.

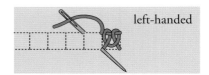

left-handed

❶ *Left-handers work this stitch in mirror image, from left to right.*

knotted pearl stitch

This stitch is also known as *reverse Palestrina knot stitch*. It can also be worked turned 90 degrees anticlockwise.

1 Use two guides. Bring the thread out between them. A short way above, take a horizontal stitch from the right to the left line.

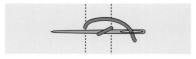

2 Pull the needle through. Slide the needle horizontally from the right under the first stitch.
❶ *Do not enter the fabric.*

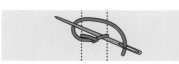

3 From below, slide the needle under the first stitch's right half, and over the working thread.
❶ *Do not enter the fabric.*

4 Pull the needle through to create a small neat knot. A little way above, take a horizontal stitch from the right to the left line.

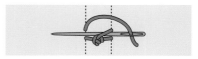

5 Pull the needle through. Slide the needle horizontally from the right under the previous stitch, without entering the fabric.

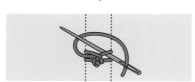

6 From below, slide the needle under the previous stitch's right half, and over the working thread.

7 Continue in the same way to build up a line of stitching.

left-handed

❶ *Left-handers work this stitch turned 180 degrees.*

parma stitch

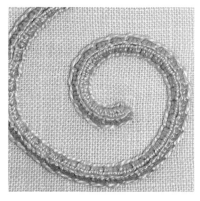

Parma stitch comes from a regional embroidery in Parma, Italy. It is traditionally worked in cream or white on natural coloured linen. For contemporary use, the two layers can be contrasting or the same colour.

1 Work a foundation of three rows of chain stitch, with each row in the same direction, and the stitches in each row aligning with those in the other rows.

❶ *When working around a curve, the stitches on the inner side of the curve should be shorter, and the stitches on the outer side of the curve should be longer, so that they all still align.*

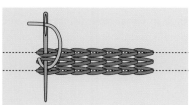

2 Change to a tapestry needle. Bring a new thread out at the left end, between the top two rows. Make a buttonhole stitch under both the bottom half of the top row's first chain, and the top half of the middle row's first chain.

❶ *Do not enter the fabric at any time during the stitching of this layer.*

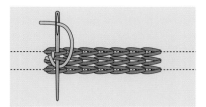

3 Pull the needle through. Work another buttonhole stitch next to the first one, in the first chains.

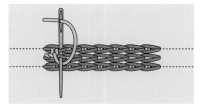

4 Pull the needle through. Work a third stitch next to the second one, in the first chains.

❶ *Each set of chains will have three buttonhole stitches worked into them.*

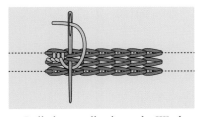

5 Pull the needle through. Work a buttonhole stitch in the bottom half of the top row's second chain, and the top half of the middle row's second chain.

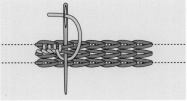

6 Pull the needle through. Work another buttonhole stitch next to the first one, into the same chain stitches.

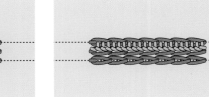

7 Continue working three buttonholes in each set of chains in the row. Take the thread through to the back to finish the row.

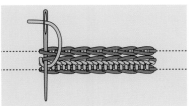

8 Turn the work 180 degrees. Bring a new thread out on the left, between the top and middle chain rows. Work a buttonhole stitch as before.

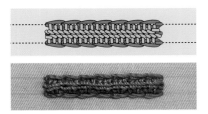

9 Continue working three buttonholes in each set of chains in the row. Take the thread through to the back to finish the row.

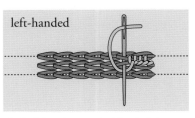

left-handed

❶ *Left-handers work this stitch in mirror image.*

pearl stitch

This stitch creates a raised, beaded line of knots which can be close together or spaced apart. Working with a thick thread such as perle thread will show off this stitch to its best effect.

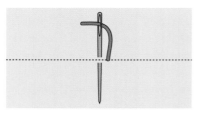

1 Use one guide. Bring the thread out on the line. A little to the left, take a very short stitch from just above the line to just below.

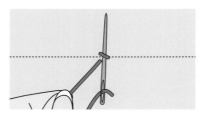

2 Pull the needle through. From below, insert the needle under the stitch, without entering the fabric. Hold the emerging thread in your left hand to maintain tension.

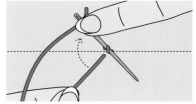

3 Still holding the thread, use your right forefinger to push the eye of the needle around in a clockwise direction.

❶ *This twists the stitch.*

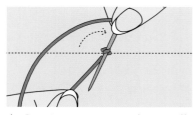

4 Continue rotating the needle until the tip points to seven o'clock.

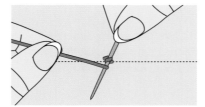

5 Take the thread in your left hand down to the right behind the needle, then over the front.

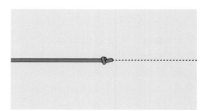

6 Still holding the thread in your left hand to maintain tension, pull the needle through, to create a neat knot.

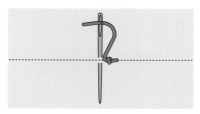

7 With the same spacing and stitch length as before, take a stitch from above the line to just below.

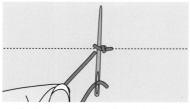

8 Pull the needle through. From below, insert the needle under the stitch without entering the fabric. Hold the emerging thread in your left hand to maintain tension.

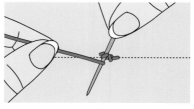

9 Turn the needle in a clockwise direction until the point is at seven o'clock. Take the thread in your left hand down to the right behind the needle, then over the front.

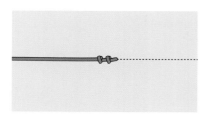

10 Still holding the thread in your left hand to maintain tension, pull the needle through, to create a neat knot.

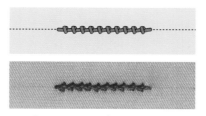

11 Continue in the same way to build up a line of stitching.

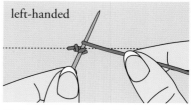

left-handed

❶ *Left-handers work this stitch rotated 180 degrees, travelling from left to right.*

pin stitch

This decorative stitch is used for appliqué and creates small holes along the appliquéd shape's edge. It is usually employed with fine, lightweight fabrics such as voile and muslin. Madeira embroidery features pin stitch appliqué.

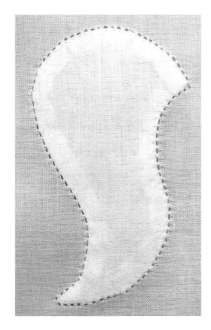

1 Bring the thread out through the edge of the appliqué shape. Next to that, take a very short stitch into the base fabric, parallel with the shape's edge.

2 Pull the needle through. Insert it in the same hole as before, bringing it out through both layers of fabric at the edge of the appliqué shape, level with the end of the first stitch.

3 Pull the needle through, and tighten the stitch to create small holes at each end of the first stitch.

4 Insert the needle into the hole at the end of the first stitch, and using the same stitch length as before take a very short stitch into the base fabric, parallel with the shape's edge.

5 Pull the needle through. Insert it in the same hole as before, bringing it out through both layers of fabric at the edge of the appliqué shape, level with the end of the last stitch.

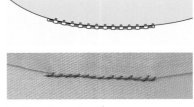

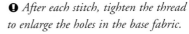

6 Continue in the same way to build up a line of stitching.
❶ *After each stitch, tighten the thread to enlarge the holes in the base fabric.*

left-handed

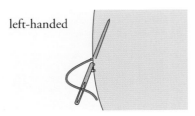

❶ *Left-handers work this stitch rotated 90 degrees clockwise.*

plaited braid stitch

Regarded as a difficult stitch, if one practises this stitch until it becomes a rhythm, it is attractive and rewarding. Thread that has body is easier to manipulate. Metallic thread is ideal, and is what it would have been used in Elizabethan times when this stitch was most common.

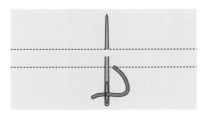

1 Use two guides. Bring the thread out on the lower line. A little left, take a vertical stitch from just above the centre, coming out on the top line.

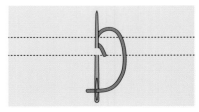

2 Pull the needle through. Level with the previous stitch, and using the same stitch length as before, take a short stitch from the lower line to just below the centre.

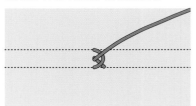

3 Pull the needle through, keeping the previous stitch in a gentle curve.

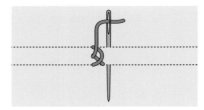

4 A little to the right, take a stitch from the top to the bottom line.

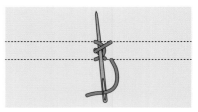

5 Insert the needle at the centre, left of the curved stitch. Slide it under the two crossing threads at the top: the previous stitch and the top part of the curved stitch.
❶ *Do not enter the fabric.*

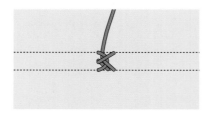

6 Pull the needle through.

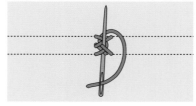

7 Without entering the fabric, slide the needle from below under the three crossing threads at the bottom: the very first stitch, the curved stitch and the previous stitch. Bring the needle out centrally, left of the curved stitch.

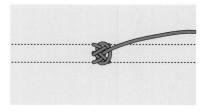

8 Pull the needle through, leaving the stitch curving gently.
❶ *The curve should sit over the ends of the previous stitches.*

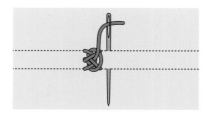

9 A little to the right, take a stitch from the top to the bottom line.
❶ *Start new threads at this point. Take the old thread to the back on the top line, and bring out the new thread on the bottom line.*

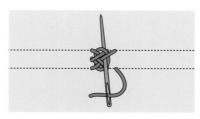

10 Insert the needle left of the last curved stitch. Slide it under the last three crossing threads at the top: the curved stitch, the previous stitch and the prior diagonal stitch.
❶ *Do not enter the fabric.*

11 Pull the needle through.

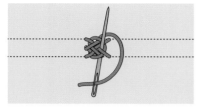

12 Without entering the fabric, slide the needle from below under the three crossing threads at the bottom: the previous stitch, the curved stitch and the prior diagonal stitch. Bring the needle out centrally, left of the curved stitch.

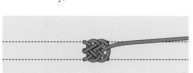

13 Pull the needle through, leaving the previous stitch hanging down in a gentle curve.
❶ *Use the same tension as before.*

14 Continue cycling through steps 9 to 13 to build up a line of stitching. To finish, take a small stitch over the final curved stitch.

❶ *The back of the work is a series of parallel lines stretching between the two guide lines.*

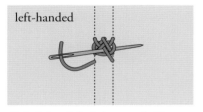

left-handed

❶ *Left-handed stitchers work this stitch turned 90 degrees clockwise, travelling from top to bottom.*

stitch spacing

Spacing (lengthwise, not width between the lines) affects the appearance. The left and middle examples are well spaced, but the right one is too squashed compared to historical examples. To check spacing, look at the distance between the stitches on the back.

thread thickness

If the thread is too thin it looks gappy (left). Don't use shorter spacing to try to cover for it (centre left). Instead reduce the width and length of the stitching (centre right) or use a thicker thread to give better coverage (right).

working curves

For curves, the stitch spacing and angle are adjusted. On the outside edge of a curve, the stitches are spaced apart further. On an inside curve edge the spacing is reduced. The back is shown on the right.

working a point

To work a point, for such a wide stitch it is best to butt the ends together. Finish the part coming up to the corner, then start a new line level with the edge of the previous stitching.

joining lines at an angle

To join lines at a sharp angle, the stitching starts narrow and widens out (or vice versa for an end) over a very short distance. Joins on the left or right will be different due to the stitch structure.

queen stitch

Also known as *Rococo stitch*, this stitch can be worked singly or in rows as a filling.

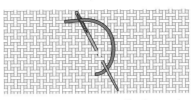

1 Using a tapestry needle, bring the thread out. Insert the needle four threads above. Bring it out one thread right and two down. Take the thread under the needle point.

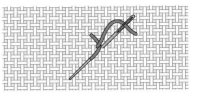

2 Pull the needle through, and tighten the stitch making small holes at the stitch's top and bottom. Insert the needle one thread to the right, on the other side of the stitch. Bring it out through the bottom hole.

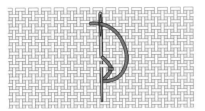

3 Pull the needle through. Insert the needle at the top, bringing it out two threads below. Keep the working thread right of the needle.

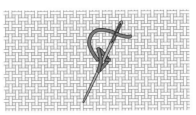

4 Pull the needle through and gently tighten the stitch. Insert the needle one thread to the right on the other side of the stitch. Bring it out at the bottom.

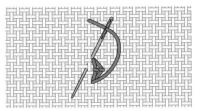

5 Pull the needle through. Insert the needle at the top, bringing it out one thread left and two down. Keep the working thread right of the needle.

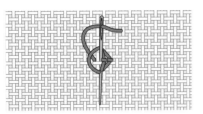

6 Pull the needle through, leaving the stitch still loose. Insert the needle one thread right, on the other side of the loose stitch. Bring it out at the bottom.

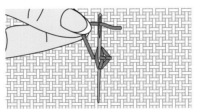

7 Leaving the needle in the fabric, gently pull the thread to tighten the stitch around the needle.

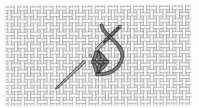

8 Pull the needle through. Insert the needle at the top, bringing it out two threads left and down. Keep the working thread right of the needle.

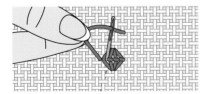

9 Pull the needle through and insert the needle one thread right, over the stitch. Gently pull to tighten the stitch around the needle.

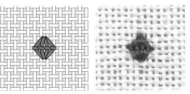

10 Take the needle through to the back to complete the stitch.

left-handed

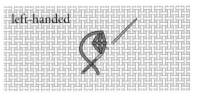

❶ *Left-handers work this stitch rotated 180 degrees.*

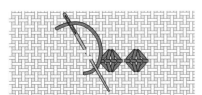

❶ *For subsequent stitches, bring the needle out four threads left of the last stitch's bottom, and work as before.*

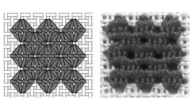

❶ *Subsequent rows fit into the gaps of the previous rows so that there is no space between.*

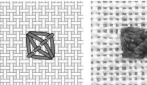

❶ *Queen stitch can also be worked on the diagonal.*

raised fishbone stitch

This stitch makes an excellent raised filling for leaves and other long narrow shapes. To make the stitches look like veins on a leaf, begin stitching at the leaf tip (not the stem end) because otherwise the veins will go the wrong way on the leaf. Also known as *overlapping herringbone stitch*.

1 Use a leaf shape with a centre vein. Bring the thread out at the leaf tip. Insert the needle in the centre vein some way down. Bring the needle out on the edge of the leaf, to the left of where the thread emerged.

2 Pull the needle through. From the right, take a short stitch from one side of the centre vein to the other, just below the end of the first stitch.

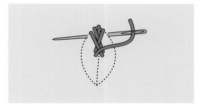

3 Pull the needle through. Take a stitch on the leaf edge from just right of the first stitch, to just left of the top of the previous stitch.

4 Pull the needle through. From the right, take a stitch from one side of the centre vein to the other, just below the ends of the previous stitches.

5 Take a stitch from the right leaf edge, just below the previous right stitch, to the left leaf edge just below the previous left stitch.

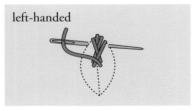

left-handed

6 Continue in the same manner to fill the leaf shape. Finish by taking the needle into the fabric on the lower right edge.

❶ *Left-handers work this stitch in mirror image.*

rhodes stitch

This stitch has a raised appearance due to the build up of many crossing threads in the centre.

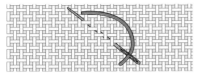

1 Bring a tapestry needle out. Insert it five threads right and down, bringing it out one thread below where it first emerged.

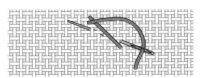

2 Pull the needle through. Insert it one thread above the right end of the previous stitch, bringing it out one thread below where it last emerged.

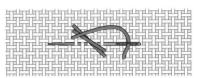

3 Pull the needle through. Insert it one thread above the right end of the previous stitch, bringing it out one thread below where it last emerged.

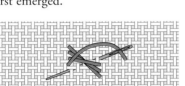

4 Pull the needle through. Insert it one thread above the end of the previous stitch, bringing it out one thread below where it last emerged.

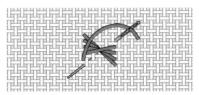

5 Pull the needle through. Insert it one thread above the end of the previous stitch, bringing it out one thread below where it last emerged, in the corner.

6 Pull the needle through. Insert it in the corner, one thread above the end of the previous stitch, bringing it out one thread right where it last emerged.

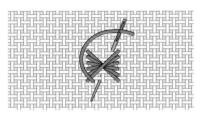

7 Pull the needle through. Insert it one thread left of the end of the previous stitch, bringing it out one thread right where it last emerged.

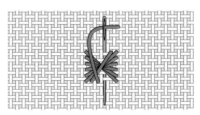

8 Pull the needle through. Insert it one thread left of the end of the previous stitch, bringing it out one thread right where it last emerged.

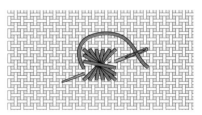

9 Turn the work 90 degrees clockwise to assist with inserting the needle. Pull the needle through. Insert it one thread above the end of the previous stitch, bringing it out one below where it last emerged.

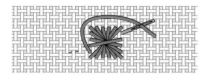

10 Pull the needle through. Take the thread to the back one thread above the end of the previous stitch.

11 Turn the work 90 degrees for the final effect.

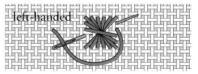

❶ *Left-handers work this stitch rotated 180 degrees.*

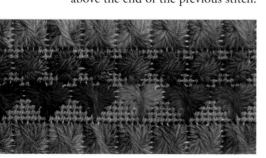

❶ *Rhodes stitch can be worked over any number of threads, and the corners can also be cut off to create a more circular or octagonal appearance.*

❶ *Other shapes such as hearts can also be created using Rhodes stitch.*

half rhodes stitch

Half Rhodes stitch can be worked singly or as a filling.

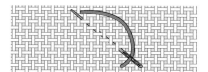

1 Bring a tapestry needle out. Insert it six threads right and five down. Bring it out one below where it first emerged.
❶ *When working half Rhodes stitch as a filling, it must span an even number of threads in order to work properly.*

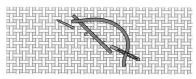

2 Pull the needle through. Insert it one thread above the right end of the previous stitch, bringing it out one thread below where it last emerged.

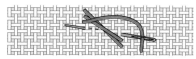

3 Pull the needle through. Insert it one thread above the right end of the previous stitch, bringing it out one thread below where it last emerged.

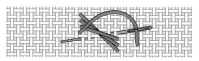

4 Pull the needle through. Insert it one thread above the end of the previous stitch, bringing it out one thread below where it last emerged.

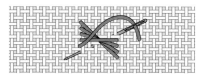

5 Pull the needle through. Insert it one thread above the end of the previous stitch, bringing it out one thread below where it last emerged.

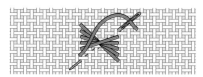

6 Pull the needle through. Insert it one thread above the end of the previous stitch. Bring it out one below where it last emerged, in the corner.

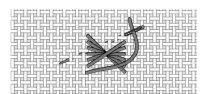

7 Pull the needle through. Insert it one thread above the end of the previous stitch. Bring it out four threads down and nine to the left.
❶ *To finish a single half Rhodes stitch, take the thread to the back and secure it.*

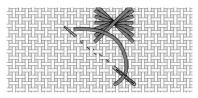

8 Pull the needle through. Insert it six threads right and five down. Bring it out one thread below the emerging thread.

9 Pull the needle through. Insert it one thread above the right end of the previous stitch, bringing it out one thread below where it last emerged.

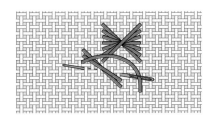

10 Pull the needle through. Insert it one thread above the right end of the previous stitch, bringing it out one thread below where it last emerged.

11 Continue in the same way to build down a line of half Rhodes stitches.

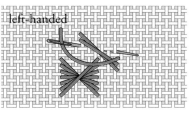

left-handed

❶ *Left-handers work this stitch rotated 180 degrees.*

rope stitch

This wide, slanting stitch, has a raised edge on one side.

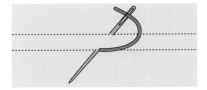

1 Use two guides. Bring the thread out on the lower line. Diagonally insert the needle from the top to the bottom line, next to the emerging thread.

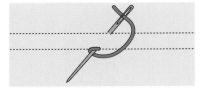

2 Take the thread left over the front of the needle and up behind the needle point.

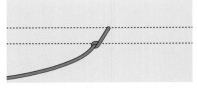

3 Pull the needle through.

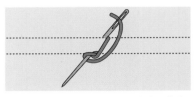

4 Insert the needle just left of the previous stitch. Bring it out right next to the top. Wrap the thread around the needle point.
❶ *Allow no gaps between stitches.*

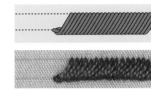

5 Continue in the same way. Take a short stitch to anchor the final stitch.

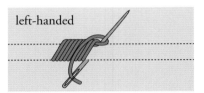

left-handed

❶ *Left-handers work this stitch rotated 180 degrees.*

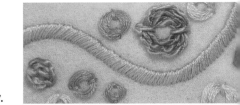

rosette stitch

This pretty rose stitch is not very stable. Treat it delicately.

1 Bring the thread out. Take a vertical stitch, bringing the needle out where it first emerged.
❶ *Do not pull the needle through.*

2 Wind the thread anticlockwise under the ends of the needle.
❶ *The thread should be loosely looped to give it a rounded shape.*

3 Continue winding until it is the desired size.
❶ *Make sure that each wrap sits next to the previous one, without any overlaps.*

4 Place a pin in the 'elbow' just above the wraps, on the right side of the needle.

5 Carefully pull the needle through, without moving the wraps.

6 With the pin still in place at the top, take the thread through to the back at the base of the rosette.

7 Bring the needle out next to the pin, inside the last wrap.

8 Take a short stitch over the last wrap to finish. Remove the pin.

left-handed

❶ *Left-handers turn the work 90 degrees anticlockwise.*

running stitch

Running stitch, also known as *basting*, is one of the most simple stitches. It can be used as a linear or filling stitch.

1 Use one guide. Bring the thread out on it. With regular spacing, insert the needle point in and out several times on the line.
❶ *The stitches are often slightly longer on top of the fabric than underneath.*

2 Pull the needle through so that the stitches lie flat against the fabric.
❶ *Do not pull too tightly or the fabric may pucker.*

3 Using the same spacing and stitch length as before, insert the needle in and out several times on the line.

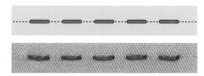

4 Pull the needle through so that the stitches lie flat on the fabric. To finish, take the needle through to the back at the end of a stitch.

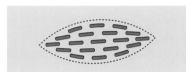

❶ *To fill shapes, work lines of running stitch.*

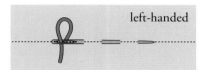

left-handed

❶ *Left-handers work this stitch in mirror image, from left to right.*

whipped running stitch

This stitch, also known as *cordonnet stitch*, is most effective when worked with contrasting thread colours.

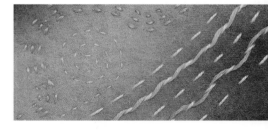

1 Work a foundation of running stitch. With a tapestry needle, bring a new thread out from the bottom of the right-most stitch. Slide the needle from above under the next stitch.
❶ *Do not enter the fabric.*

2 Pull the needle through. Without entering the fabric, slide the needle from above under the next stitch.

3 Continue in the same way to whip all the running stitch. To finish, take the thread to the back under the centre of the last stitch, from above.
❶ *Left-handers work this stitch rotated 180 degrees.*

threaded running stitch

Threaded running stitch is most effective when worked with contrasting thread colours.

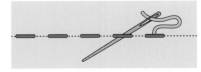

1 Work a foundation of running stitch. Using a tapestry needle, bring a new thread out from the top of the right-most stitch. Slide the needle from above under the next stitch.
❶ *Do not enter the fabric.*

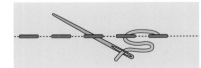

2 Pull the needle through. Without entering the fabric, slide the needle from below under the next stitch.

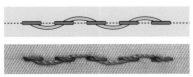

3 Continue taking the needle under the stitches from alternate sides. To finish, take the thread through to the back under the centre of the final stitch.
❶ *Left-handers work this stitch in mirror image.*

burden stitch (running stitch version)

This is the second type of Burden stitch. It is a running stitch and the other is a couched stitch (see page 67). This stitch is a very economical way of filling a shape as nearly all of the thread lies on the surface of the fabric. Each stitch goes under only a few fabric threads.

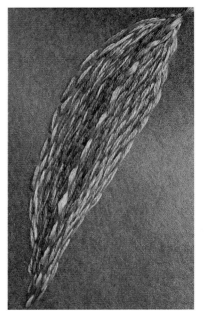

1 Bring the thread out on the line. Insert the needle point in and out several times on the line, passing under a few fabric threads each time the needle goes under the fabric.
❶ *The stitches should be long on top and very short underneath.*

2 Pull the needle through so that the stitches lie flat on the fabric, but do not pucker. Using the same spacing as before, insert the needle point in and out several times on the line.

3 Pull the needle through. To finish the line, take the needle through to the back at the end of a stitch.

4 Turn the work 180 degrees to allow comfortable insertion of the needle. Just above the first line, work new stitches so that the needle enters the fabric level with the centre of the previous line's stitches.
❶ *The first stitch will be slightly shorter than half the usual stitch length.*

5 Complete the remainder of the line, finishing level with the end of the previous line's stitches.
❶ *The stitches form a brick pattern.*

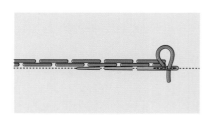

6 Turn the work 180 degrees again. Using the same stitch length and spacing as the first line, work running stitches, below the previous line.

7 Continue working lines of running stitch in a brick pattern to fill the shape.

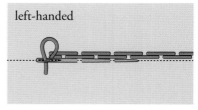

left-handed

❶ *Left-handers work this stitch in mirror image, from left to right.*

130

holbein stitch

The painter Hans Holbein often depicted this stitch on his portrait subjects' clothing. It is reversible, appearing the same on the front and back, and is an important part of Assisi embroidery and Spanish blackwork. It can be worked as both counted and surface embroidery. Also called *chiara stitch*, *double running stitch*, *line stitch*, *Roumanian stitch*, *square stitch*, *stroke stitch*, *two-sided line stitch* and *two-sided stroke stitch*.

1 Use one guide. Bring the thread out on it. Insert the needle point in and out several times on the line.
❶ *The stitches should be the same length on the fabric's front and back.*

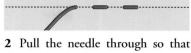

2 Pull the needle through so that the stitches lie flat against the fabric.
❶ *Do not pull too tightly or the fabric may pucker.*

3 Using the same spacing and stitch length as before, insert the needle in and out several times on the line.

4 Continue until the desired length of stitching is achieved.

5 Turn the work 180 degrees to aid with insertion of the needle. Insert the needle at exactly the end of the last stitch, bringing it in and out through the same holes as the ends of the existing stitches, to fill the gaps.

6 Pull the needle through.

7 Continue filling between the previous stitches to complete the line.

working a side journey

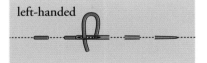

left-handed

❶ *Left-handers work this stitch in mirror image, from left to right.*

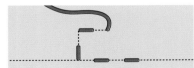

1 Stitch to the junction of the side path. Turn off and continue with the same stitch spacing and length.

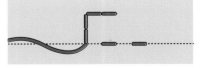

2 Work back along the side path to the main path, filling the spaces between the stitches.

3 Stitch along to the end of the main path.

4 Work back along the main path to fill the gaps between the stitches.

satin stitch

Satin stitch is a beautiful filling stitch, also known as *damask stitch*. Satin stitches longer than about 2cm (¾in) will not sit properly. If the area to be filled is larger than this, divide it into smaller sections, or use another stitch.

Mount the fabric in a hoop or frame to avoid puckering. Satin stitch can be difficult: obtaining smooth curves, edges and surface, and keeping the stitches parallel. Practise will be required to master this stitch.

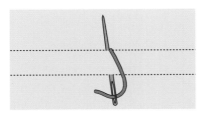

1 Use two guides. Bring the thread out on the top line. Insert the needle directly below, on the lower line. Bring the needle out right next to the emerging thread on the top line.
❶ *Stitches should be very close together.*

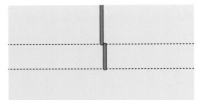

2 Pull the needle through and tighten the stitch so that it lays straight and flat upon the surface.
❶ *Too tight and the fabric will pucker; if too loose, the stitch will curve. Constant tension will prevent lumps.*

3 Right next to the first stitch, insert the needle from the bottom to the top line.
❶ *Stitches are always made in the same direction: coming up on the same line, going down on the opposite line.*

4 Continue working closely spaced stitches to fill the shape.

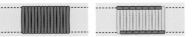

❶ *Never work back and forth across the shape (front shown left, back shown right). The stitches will curve slightly, and not sit properly.*

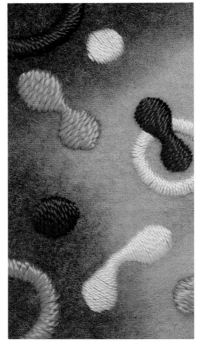

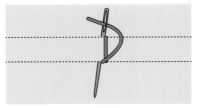

❶ *Bringing the needle up on the near side of the shape and inserting it on the far side can sometimes give better results. Either way is acceptable, but do not change direction midway.*

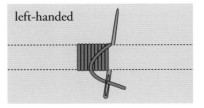

left-handed

❶ *Left-handers work this stitch in mirror image.*

creating a smooth surface

The best way to ensure a smooth surface is to use only one strand of thread. It does take longer, but it provides much better results.

Multiple strands will twist around each other, creating lumps.

If the thread you are using tends to untwist (as shown above), retwist it so that the twist remains constant across all stitches.

maintaining stitch angle

Pale or removable guide lines drawn within the stitching area can assist in keeping stitches parallel.

dealing with shaped ends

Attractive tapered or rounded ends can be difficult to achieve. It is best to start in the centre and work outwards.

maintaining stitch angle between non-parallel edges

At the top left edge of the leaf, the stitch ends are well spaced apart. At the top right edge, the space between the stitch ends is much shorter. Along the centre vein, the spaces between stitch ends are constant as the vein slope also remains constant.

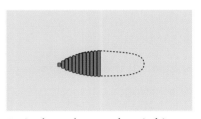

In this example you can see what happens if the distance between the stitch ends is kept constant along the edge of the leaf. The stitches splay out at odd angles, looking much less pleasing.

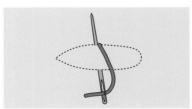

1 Begin at the centre and work towards one end.

3 Turn the work 180 degrees. Bring the needle out at the centre on the opposite side to before, and work out to the other end.

❶ *Stitch direction remains constant.*

2 At the end, taper the stitching to fit the shape.

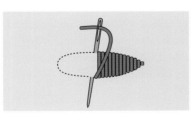

4 At the end, taper the stitching to fit the shape.

curving satin stitch

When working satin stitch round curves, careful stitch placement is necessary to form a smooth surface, with no gaps between stitches on the outer edge of the curve. Tight curves need more adjusting than shallow curves.

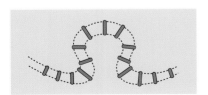

For curving shapes, stitchers generally aim for the stitches to sit across the stitching area, perpendicular to the sides.

❶ *Key stitch angles are shown above.*

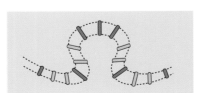

It can be difficult to fit the stitches into very tight curves. It can help if the stitch angles compensate a little in adjoining areas.

❶ *Adjusted stitches shown in green.*

Work the curves, adjusting the stitch angle as necessary, cramming stitches into the inner curves, and fanning them at the curve's outer edges.

❶ *Ensure the outer curve edges have sufficient coverage of the fabric.*

padded satin stitch

Padding satin stitch provides depth and can also assist with creating very smooth edges. For this reason, padded satin stitch often gives a more pleasing result than regular satin stitch. Use a thick thread to build up the padding more quickly. The padding and satin stitch should be worked in the same colour, so that the padding won't show accidentally. There are a number of different ways to pad satin stitch, and they can also be used to pad other stitches such as buttonhole stitch.

split stitch padding

Split stitch the easiest form of padding. Compared to some of the other padding methods, it produces a very flat result.

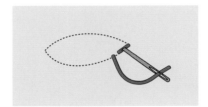

1 Using split stitch or split back stitch, outline the shape. Work so that the edge of the stitches sits right on the inside of the line.

2 The completed padding.

running stitch padding

1 Outline the shape using a running stitch where most of the thread sits on the fabric's surface. Work so that the edge of the stitches sits right on the inside of the line.

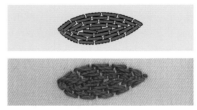

2 Continuing on, fill the rest of the shape by spiralling inwards.

❶ *Work additional layers for extra height. Step them half a stitch width inwards so that each layer is slightly smaller than previous ones. This gives a rounded shape to the padding edges.*

satin stitch padding

Layers of satin stitch worked at right angles to the preceding layer can be used to create padding.

Work a layer of satin stitch padding, perpendicular to the planned direction of the top layer's stitches.

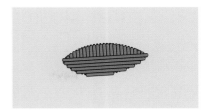

For more than one layer of padding, the the top padding layer must be stitched perpendicular to the final satin stitches. Each preceding layer is perpendicular to the layer directly above.

chain stitch padding

Chain stitch padding creates a firm, stable padded base.

1 Outline the shape in chain stitch so that the outside edge of the chain stitch sits just inside the shape edge.

2 Fill the centre with additional rows of chain stitch.

❶ *Work additional layers for extra height. Step them half a stitch width inwards so that each layer is slightly smaller than previous ones. This gives a rounded shape to the padding edges.*

working satin stitch over padding

1 Bring the needle out at the edge of the shape, just under the edge of the chain stitching.
❶ *When working shaped ends, start at the centre as shown. Otherwise, start at one end and work along to the other.*

2 Insert the needle on the opposite side, just under the edge of the chain stitch.
❶ *This slightly conceals the stitch ends, smoothing the edge.*

❶ *Slightly concealing the ends of each stitch under the edge of the padding stitches gives a cleaner edge to the shape. The diagram above shows a cross-section of how the stitching would appear, when looking across the surface of the fabric.*

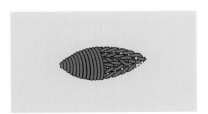

3 Continue working satin stitch over the top of the chain stitch padding, out to one end.

4 Turn the work 180 degrees. Bring the needle out at the centre on the opposite side to before, and work towards the other end.

5 The completed padded satin stitch.
❶ *Left-handers work this stitch in mirror image.*

satin stitch kloster blocks

Kloster blocks are the basic building blocks of Hardanger embroidery and consist of five parallel satin stitches worked over a block of four by four fabric threads.

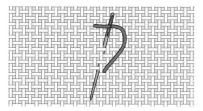

1 Bring a tapestry needle out. Insert it four threads above. Bring it out one thread left of the emerging thread.

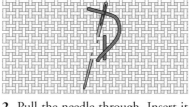

2 Pull the needle through. Insert it four threads above. Bring it out one thread left of the emerging thread.

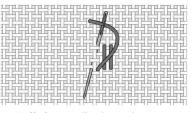

3 Pull the needle through. Insert it four threads above. Bring it out one thread left of the emerging thread.

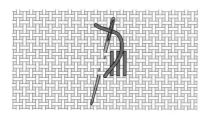

4 Pull the needle through. Insert it four threads above. Bring it out one thread left of the emerging thread.

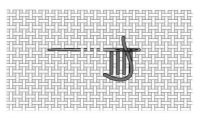

5 Pull the needle through. Insert it four threads above. Bring it out four threads to the left.

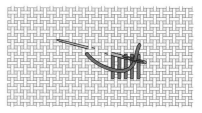

6 Pull the needle through. Insert it four threads right, bringing it out one thread above the emerging thread.

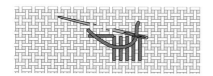

7 Pull the needle through. Insert it four threads right, bringing it out one thread above the emerging thread.

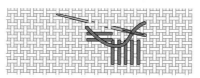

8 Pull the needle through. Insert it four threads right, bringing it out one thread above the emerging thread.

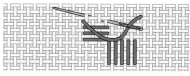

9 Pull the needle through. Insert it four threads right, bringing it out one thread above the emerging thread.

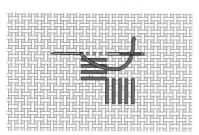

10 Pull the needle through. Insert it four threads right, bringing it out in the same hole as the emerging thread.

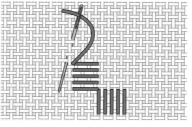

11 Pull the needle through. Insert it four threads above. Bring it out one thread left of the emerging thread.

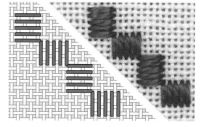

12 Continue in the same way to build up a line of kloster blocks.

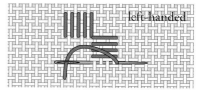

❶ *Left-handers work this stitch turned 180 degrees.*

scottish stitch

Scottish stitch has squares of diagonal stitches, consisting of five stitches over three by three fabric threads. Use a tapestry needle.

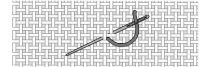

1 Bring the needle out. Insert it one thread up and right. Bring it out again two threads left and one down.

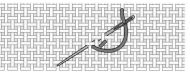

2 Pull the needle through. Insert it two threads up and right. Bring it out three threads left and two down.

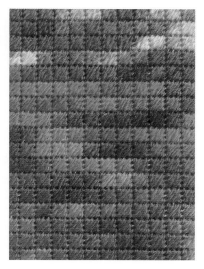

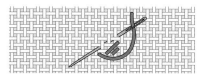

3 Pull the needle through. Insert it three threads up and right. Bring it out three threads left and two down.

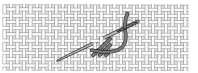

4 Pull the needle through. Insert it two threads up and right. Bring it out two threads left and one down.

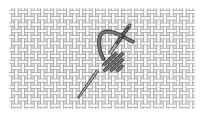

5 Pull the needle through. Insert it one thread up and right. Bring it out two threads left and three down.

6 Pull the needle through. Insert it one thread up and right. Bring it out again two threads left and one down.

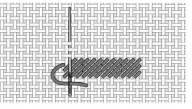

7 Continue in the same way to build down a line of stitching. To start the next row, insert the needle to finish the last stitch of the row and bring it out three threads up.

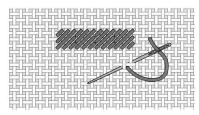

8 Turn the work 180 degrees. Pull the needle through. Insert it one thread up and right. Bring it out again two thread left and one down.

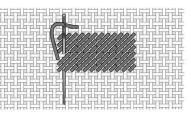

9 Continue in the same way to build down a line of stitching. To start the next row, insert the needle to finish the last stitch of the row and bring it out three threads up.

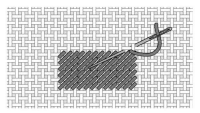

10 Turn the work 180 degrees. Pull the needle through. Insert it one thread up and right. Bring it out again two thread left and one down.

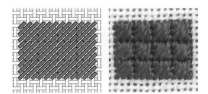

11 Continue in the same way to complete the row of stitches.

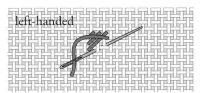

left-handed

❶ *Left-handers work this stitch rotated 180 degrees.*

scroll stitch

Scroll stitch is a very rhythmic stitch of swirls and waves. It creates a lovely scalloped line, and suits straight lines or gentle curves. It is not, however, a very stable stitch. Also known as *single knotted line stitch*.

1 Use one guide. Bring the thread out on the line. A little to the right, insert the needle diagonally from above right, from one side of the line to the other.

❶ *The stitch should be very short.*

2 With the working thread in hand, take it right under the back end of the needle.

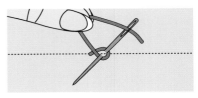

3 Continue winding the thread, taking it under the front end of the needle. Tighten the thread around the needle.

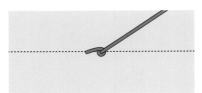

4 Pull the needle through to the right.

❶ *Do not pull the stitch too tight or the scroll effect will be lost.*

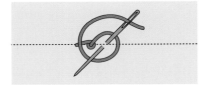

5 Moving right, diagonally insert the needle to make a short stitch from one side of the line to the other. Wind the thread around the needle in a clockwise direction.

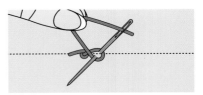

6 Tighten the thread around the needle.

7 Continue working in the same way to build up a line of stitching.

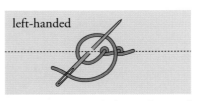

left-handed

❶ *Left-handers work this stitch rotated 180 degrees.*

seed stitch

Seed stitch is a filling stitch made up of small randomly scattered stitches. It is also known as *isolated back stitch*, *seed filling stitch*, *seeding stitch*, and *speckling stitch*.

1 Bring the thread up through the fabric. Take the thread to the back close by, to make a very short stitch.

2 Make another stitch of the same length, close by, at a different angle.

 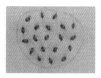

3 Fill the shape with very short, randomly scattered and angled stitches.

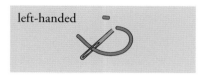

left-handed

❶ *Left-handers insert their needle from the left, rather than the right.*

double seed stitch

Each stitch is worked twice to create thicker 'seeds'.

1 Bring the thread up through the fabric. Make a short stitch, coming out where the thread first emerged.

2 Pull the needle through. Take the thread to the back at the end of the first stitch, to create a double seed stitch.

3 Make another stitch of the same length, close by, at a different angle.

4 Pull the needle through. Take the thread to the back at the end of the stitch.

5 Fill the shape with very short, double, randomly scattered and angled stitches.

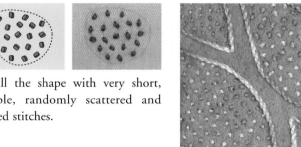

seed stitch variation

1 Bring the thread up through the fabric. Take the thread to the back close by, to make a very short stitch.

2 Bring the needle up adjacent to the stitch, near one end of the stitch.

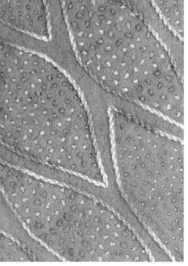

3 Insert the needle on the other side of the first stitch, near the other end.

4 Pull the needle through.
❶ *The stitch has a small 'bump' due to the second stitch which crosses over.*

5 Fill the shape as desired.

sheaf filling stitch

This stitch can be used singly, in a line, or as a filling stitch. Also known as *faggot filling stitch*.

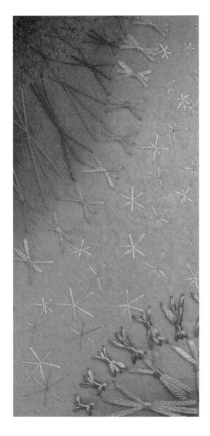

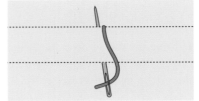

1 Use two guide lines. Bring the needle out on the top line. Insert it directly below in the bottom line. Bring the needle out on the top line a little to the left of where the thread emerged.

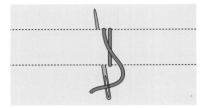

2 Pull the needle through. Insert the needle in the bottom line, directly below where the thread emerged. Bring the needle out on the top line using the same spacing as before.

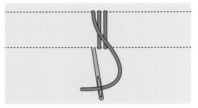

3 Pull the needle through. Take the thread to the back on the bottom line, directly below where the thread emerged.

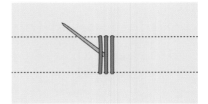

4 Bring the needle out just to the left of the middle of the centre stitch, also coming out from under the left stitch.

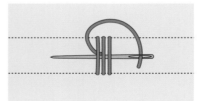

5 Slide the needle under all three stitches, from right to left, with the thread above the needle.
❶ *Do not enter the fabric.*

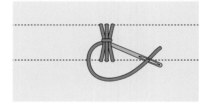

6 Pull the needle through to tighten the stitch (to make the sheaf tie). Insert the needle below the sheaf tie, under the right edge of the sheaf.

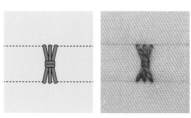

7 The completed sheaf.

left-handed

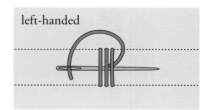

❶ *Left-handers work this stitch in mirror image.*

shisha stitch

This stitch is used to attach little round mirrors in Indian and Pakistani embroidery. Use a strong, thick thread for best effect.

1 With the mirror on the fabric surface, bring the needle out just to the right of the top. Take the thread to the back just right of the bottom.

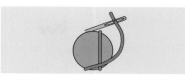

2 Bring the needle out just left of the bottom of the mirror. Take it to the back just left of the top.
❶ *The stitches need to be very tight.*

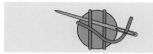

3 Bring the needle out just above the left side's middle. Slide it from the right under the near stitch, with the thread below the needle.

4 Pull the needle through and tighten the stitch. With the thread below the needle, slide it from right to left under the first stitch.

5 Pull the needle through. Take the thread through to the back just above the right side's middle.
❶ *The stitches should be very tight.*

6 Turn it 180 degrees. Bring the needle out just above the left side's middle. From the right, slide it under the near stitch, with the thread below.

7 Work across to the other side as before to complete the foundation stitches. Bring the thread out at the bottom left of the mirror.

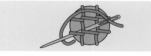

8 Slide the needle under the nearest crossed threads from above right, and over the working thread.

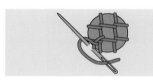

9 Pull the needle through, making a buttonhole stitch. Inserting the needle where the thread emerged, take a short stitch alongside the mirror. Take the thread under the needle point.

10 Pull the needle through, making a chain stitch. Moving anticlockwise around the foundation stitches, slide the needle under the foundation stitch and over the working thread.

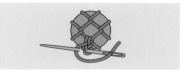

11 Insert the needle in the previous chain loop, bringing it out a short way round. Take the thread under the needle point.

12 Continue similarly, turning as needed. To finish, after a chain, slide the needle under the first chain, the beginning of the first buttonhole stitch, and the foundation stitch.

13 Take the needle over the foundation stitch, and slide it under the last stitch between where it went under the foundation stitch and the first buttonhole stitch.

14 Take the thread to the back in the crook of the last chain stitch made in step 12.

15 The completed shisha stitch.

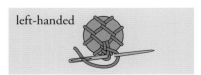

left-handed

❶ *Left-handers work this stitch in mirror image.*

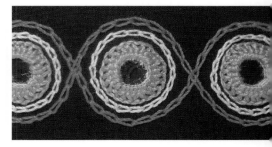

smockers' knot

This knot is often used in smocking to end off neatly and securely. However, it is also an effective knot for decorative embroidery. Because it has many loops within it, it makes a very firm, solid knot.

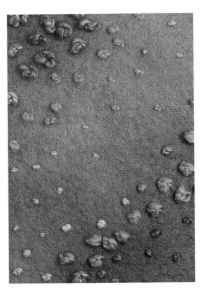

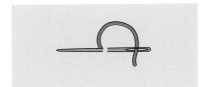

1 Bring the needle out. Take a short stitch, with the needle coming out where the thread originally emerged.

2 Pull the needle through, leaving a small loop sitting up from the fabric surface.

3 Holding the thread coming from the loop in your left hand, insert the needle in the back of the loop from right to left.

4 With the needle still in place, tighten the thread by pulling on the thread in your left hand.

5 When the thread is snug around the needle, pull the needle through the knot.
❶ *Do not pull the thread through the whole way. Leave a new loop sitting up.*

6 Holding the thread coming from the loop in your left hand, insert the needle in the back of the loop from right to left.

7 Pull the needle through the loop…

8 …and tighten to create a small neat knot.

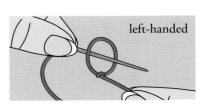

9 Take the thread through to the back at the base of the knot.

10 The completed knot.

left-handed

❶ *Left-handers work this stitch in mirror image.*

split stitch

This stitch is an excellent outlining stitch, but can also be used as a filling stitch. Two methods are shown, one is similar to stem stitch, the other is a variation on back stitch. Both produce the same result, but some stitchers may find one easier that the other. Also known as *Kensington outline stitch*.

1 Use one guide. Bring the thread out on the line, and insert the needle on the line a little way to the left.

2 Pull the needle through.

3 Bring the needle up through the centre of the last stitch, splitting it in the centre.

4 Using the same stitch length as before, insert the needle a little way to the left on the line.

5 Pull the needle through.

6 Bring the needle up through the centre of the last stitch, splitting it in the centre.

7 Continue in the same way to build up a line of stitching.

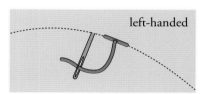

left-handed

❶ *Left-handed stitchers also work from right to left, but use their needle from the left-hand side.*

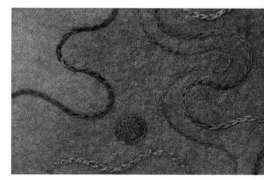

split back stitch

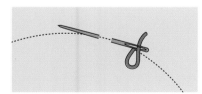

1 Use one line. Bring the needle out on the line. Insert the needle in the line one stitch length away. Bring it out half a stitch length further on.

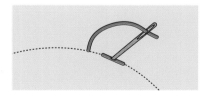

2 Pull the needle through. Insert the needle in the centre of the previous stitch, splitting it.

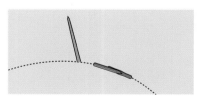

3 Pull the needle through. Bring the needle up on the line, half a stitch length from the end of the previous stitch.

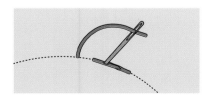

4 Pull the needle through. Insert the needle in the centre of the previous stitch, splitting it.

5 Continue in the same way, to build up a line of stitching.

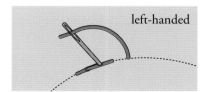

left-handed

❶ *Left-handed stitchers work in mirror image, from left to right.*

spider web stitch – whipped

Whipped spider webs create a ribbed circular shape. It can have an even or odd number of spokes. An eight-spoke web is shown below, starting with a double cross. Also called *back stitched spider's web*, *ribbed spider's web* and *ribbed wheel*.

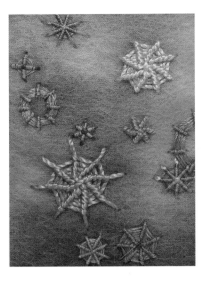

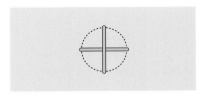

1 Using a circle as a guide, work a cross, with a stitch from the top to bottom and one from side to side.

2 Work another cross in the spaces between, with one stitch from top right to bottom left, and one from top left to bottom right.

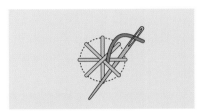

3 Using a tapestry needle, bring a new thread out between two of the spokes, just right of and below the centre. Working in an anticlockwise direction, slide the needle under the spoke that goes out to the right edge, and the one below it.

❶ *The needle should not enter the fabric during the whipping stage.*

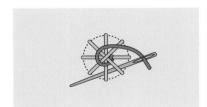

4 Pull the needle through. Slide the needle under the spoke going down to the bottom right, and the bottom spoke.

5 Pull the needle through. Slide the needle under the bottom spoke, and the next one.

6 Continue around, whipping the spokes and turning the work as necessary to assist with the insertion of the needle. To finish, take the thread through to the back when the spokes are full.

left-handed

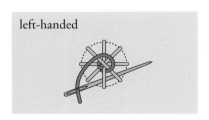

❶ *Left-handers work this stitch in mirror image, going around the spokes in an anticlockwise direction.*

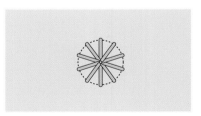

❶ *For webs with other numbers of spokes, use different quantities of crossed stitches, or work half stitches from the centre out to the edges of the circle.*

spider web stitch – woven

Woven spider webs are a raised stitch that need an odd number of spokes e.g. five, seven or nine. They can use one colour throughout or have contrasting colours for the spokes and weaving. Also known as *woven spoke stitch, woven spot* and *woven wheel*.

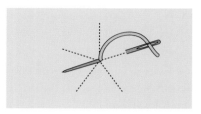

1 Use an odd number of evenly spaced lines, radiating from a central point. Bring the thread out at the centre. Insert it further out on one line, bringing it out at the centre again.

❶ *The length of the stitch determines the web's radius.*

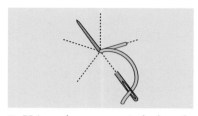

2 Using the same stitch length, work around the circle to create the remainder of the foundation stitches.

3 The completed foundation of spokes.

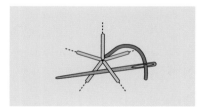

4 Change to a tapestry needle. Bring a new thread out close to the centre. Working in an anticlockwise direction, take the needle over the first spoke and under the next one.

❶ *The needle should not be inserted into the fabric at any time during the weaving stage.*

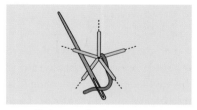

5 Pull the needle through. Take the needle over the next spoke and then under the subsequent one.

6 Pull the needle through. Take the needle over the next spoke and then under the subsequent one.

7 Continue around the spokes, weaving over and under, until the web is completely filled. To finish, take the needle through to the back.

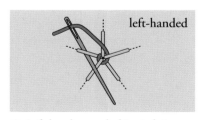

left-handed

❶ *Left-handers work this stitch in mirror image, going around the spokes in an anticlockwise direction.*

stem stitch

This is one of the most often used outline stitches, which can also be used as a filling stitch. It is also known as *crewel stitch*, *South Kensington stitch* and *stalk stitch*, and is closely related to outline stitch.

1 Use one guide line. Bring the needle out on the line. Insert it a short distance to the right.

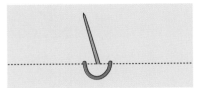

2 Pull the needle through. Leave the stitch sitting up. Bring the needle out on the line, above the stitch, and halfway along it.
❶ *Leaving the stitch sitting up assists with stitch placement.*
❶ *Always bring the needle out above the stitching.*

3 Pull the needle through and tighten the thread so that the previous stitch lies flat. Insert the needle a stitch length to the right.
❶ *The stitches half overlap each other.*

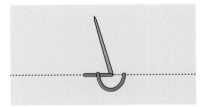

4 Pull the needle through but leave the stitch curving up gently. Bring the needle out halfway along the stitch, emerging through the same hole as the end of the first stitch.
❶ *Bring the needle out above the stitch.*

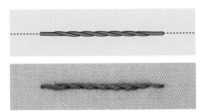

5 Continue in the same way to build up a line of stitching.

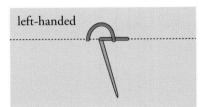

left-handed

❶ *Left-handers work this stitch rotated 180 degrees, coming out below the previous stitch.*

turning a sharp corner

1 Work up to the corner and take the thread through to the back.

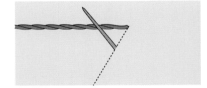

2 Bring the needle out at the far end of the next stitch, on the next side of the shape.

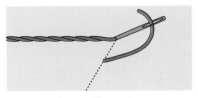

3 Insert the needle at the corner.
❶ *This backstitch fills the gap at the corner.*

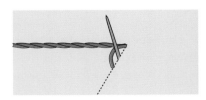

4 Bring the needle out halfway along the stitch, and continue stitching forward as before.

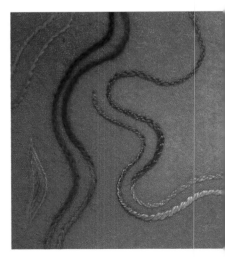

outline stitch

This stitch is the mirror image identical twin to stem stitch: it is worked similarly, but twists in the opposite direction. For left-handers, outline stitch comes out above the previous stitch, and stem comes out below.

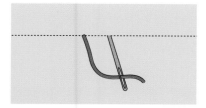

1 Use one guide. Bring the needle out on the line. Insert it a short distance to the right on the line.

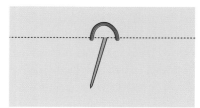

2 Pull the needle through but leave the stitch gently curving. Bring the needle out on the line, halfway along the stitch. The needle should be below the thread.

❶ *Leaving the stitch sitting up assists with stitch placement.*

❶ *Always bring the needle out below the stitching.*

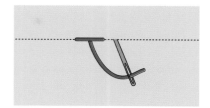

3 Pull the needle through and tighten the thread so that the previous stitch sits flat. Insert the needle a stitch length along to the right.

❶ *The stitches half overlap each other.*

4 Pull the needle through but leave the stitch curving up gently. Bring the needle out halfway along the stitch, coming out through the same hole as the end of the first stitch.

❶ *Keep the needle below the thread.*

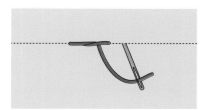

5 Pull the needle through and tighten the thread so that the previous stitch sits flat. Insert the needle a stitch length along to the right.

6 Pull the needle through but leave the stitch curving gently. Bring the needle out halfway along the stitch, coming out through the same hole as the end of the first stitch.

❶ *Keep the needle below the thread.*

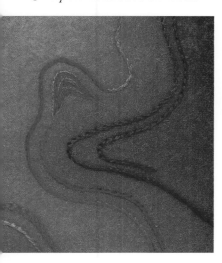

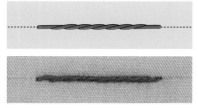

7 Continue in the same manner to build up a line of stitching.

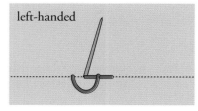

left-handed

❶ *Left-handers work this stitch turned 180 degrees, from right to left, coming out above the previous stitch.*

whipped stem stitch

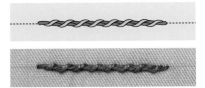

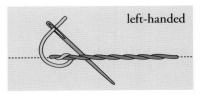

1 Work a foundation of stem stitch. Using a tapestry needle, bring the thread out above the right-most stem stitch. Without entering the fabric, slide the needle from below, under the first two stitches where they overlap.

2 Continue whipping in the same way to build up a line of stitching. To finish, take the needle through to the back under the last stem stitch.

❶ *Left-handers work this stitch rotated 180 degrees.*

portuguese knotted stem stitch

This stitch works very well on curves and produces a knotty, cord-like line.

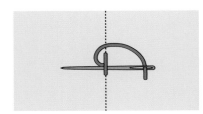

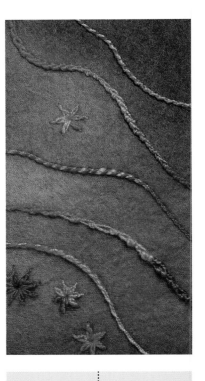

1 Use one guide. Bring the thread out on it. With the thread on the right, insert the needle further up the line. Bring it out halfway back along the stitch length.

2 Pull the needle through. With the thread at the top, slide the needle from the right under the stitch below where the thread emerged.

❶ *Do not enter the fabric.*

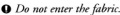

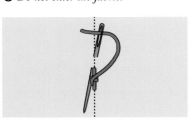

3 Without entering the fabric, take another stitch from right to left, below the previous one.

4 With the thread to the right, and the same stitch length as before, insert the needle further up the line. Bring it out at the top of the first stitch.

5 Pull the needle through. From the right, slide the needle under the over-lapping part of the two stem stitches.

❶ *Do not enter the fabric.*

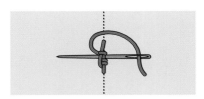

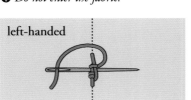

6 Take another stitch from right to left below the previous one.

7 Repeat steps 4 to 6 to build up a line of stitching. To finish, take the thread to the back at the completion of step 6.

❶ *Left-handers work this stitch in mirror image.*

raised stem stitch band

This stem stitch variation creates a smooth, high relief surface. A foundation of parallel lines is used to stem stitch over.

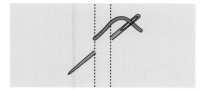

1 Use two guides. Bring the needle out on the left line. Insert the needle level with that in the right line, bringing out a little below on the left line.

2 Pull the needle through. Using the same spacing, work another stitch below.

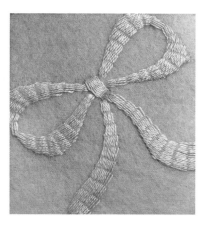

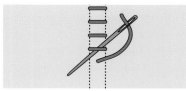

3 Continue in the same way to work the desired quantity of foundation stitches.

4 Change to a tapestry needle. Bring the needle out a little way below the top stitch, midway between the guide lines. Slide the needle under the first stitch from above. Keep the thread out of the way of the needle.

❶ *Do not enter the fabric during the whipping.*

5 Pull the needle through, towards the right, to slide the stitch across to the right.

6 Slide the needle under the next foundation stitch from above. Keep the thread out of the way of the needle.

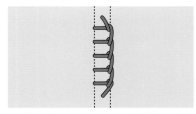

7 Continue stem stitching the remaining foundation stitches. At the end, take the thread to the back between the guides, the same stitch distance away as at the top.

8 Bring the needle out at the top, in the same hole as previously. Slide the needle under the first stitch from above. Keep the thread out of the way of the needle.

9 Continue stem stitching the remaining foundation stitches. Finish by taking the thread to the back at the bottom, in the same place as before.

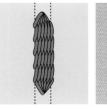

10 Fill the remaining width of the foundations stitches with more rows of stem stitch. Push the rows to the right to ensure full coverage. Start and finish each row in the same place.

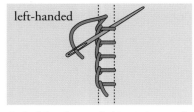

left-handed

❶ *Left-handers work this stitch rotated 180 degrees.*

149

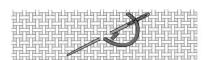

tent stitch

Also known as *canvas stitch, continental stitch, cushion stitch, needlepoint stitch* and *petit point*. Both methods look the same on the front.

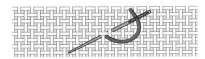

1 Bring a tapestry needle out. Insert it one thread up and right. Bring it out one thread left of the emerging thread.

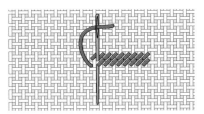

2 Pull the needle through. Insert it one thread up and right. Bring it out one left of the emerging thread.

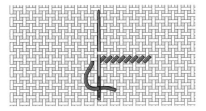

3 Continue in the same way. To start a new row, insert the needle one thread up and right, bringing it out one thread further up.

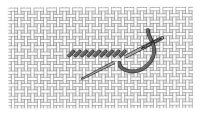

4 Turn the work 180 degrees. Pull the needle through. Insert it one thread up and right. Bring it out one thread left of the emerging thread.

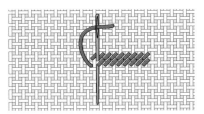

5 Continue in the same way. To start the next row, insert the needle one thread up and right, bringing it out one thread below.

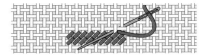

6 Turn the work 180 degrees and continue stitching.

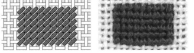

7 Continue in the same way to work rows of tent stitch.

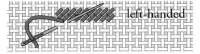

left-handed

❶ *Left-handers work this stitch rotated 180 degrees.*

diagonal tent stitch

This basketweave method is better for filling large areas as it is less likely to distort the fabric.

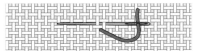

1 Bring a tapestry needle out. Insert it one thread up and right, bringing it out two threads left.

2 Pull the needle through. Insert it one thread up and right, bringing it out two threads left.

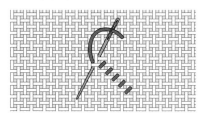

3 Continue. For a new row, insert the needle one thread up and right. Bring it out two down and one left.

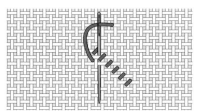

4 Pull the needle through. Insert it one thread up and right, bringing it out two threads below.

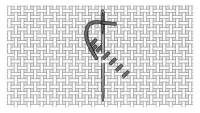

5 Pull the needle through. Insert it one thread up and right, bringing it out two threads below.

6 Continue in the same way. To start a new row, insert the needle one thread up and right. Bring it out one thread below the emerging thread.

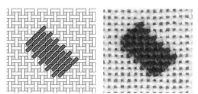

7 Follow the same pattern to work more rows of diagonal tent stitch.
❶ *The basketweave formed on the back distorts less than the first method.*

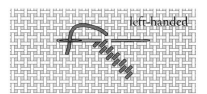

left-handed

❶ *Left-handers work this stitch rotated 180 degrees.*

150

thorn stitch

This is a couched stitch, where a long thread is tied down with crossed stitches. The laid thread can be curved or straight. The laid thread can be self-couched as shown here, or a separate thread can be used for the tying down.

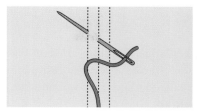

1 Use three guides. Bring the needle out at the bottom of the centre line. Quite some distance above, insert it in the centre line, bringing it out a little up on the left line.
❶ *If the laid stitch is to be curved, leave it loose enough to make the curves.*

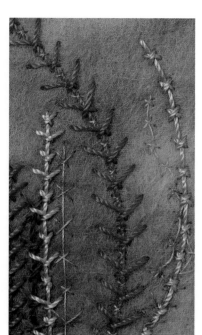

2 Pull the needle through. Take a short stitch from the right side of the laid stitch to the left side.

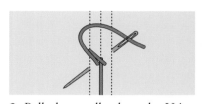

3 Pull the needle through. Using the same stitch length as before, insert the needle in the right line, level with the top of the previous stitch. Bring the needle out on the left line, below the bottom of the crossed stitches.

4 Pull the needle through. Using the same stitch length and spacing as before, take a short stitch from the right side of the laid stitch to the left side.

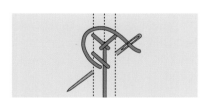

5 Pull the needle through. Using the same stitch length as before, insert the needle in the right line, level with the top of the previous stitch. Bring the needle out on the left line, below the bottom of the crossed stitches.

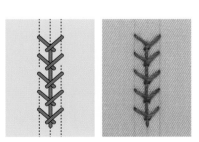

6 Continue in the same way to couch the laid thread all the way to its end.

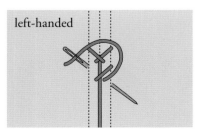

left-handed

❶ *Left-handers work this stitch in mirror image.*

trellis stitch

This detached filling stitch was used extensively in Elizabethan embroidery as a filling for motifs such as flower petals and leaves. Also known as *trellis filling stitch*.

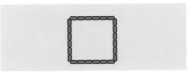

1 Outline the shape in very short back stitches. For perle 5 thread (or similar thickness) use 1.5mm (¹/₁₆in) stitches.

❶ *For thicker thread, use longer stitches, for thinner thread use shorter.*

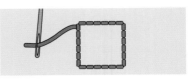

2 Change to a tapestry needle. Bring the thread out on the outside of the top stitch on the left side of the motif.

❶ *A tapestry needle lessens the chance of splitting threads.*

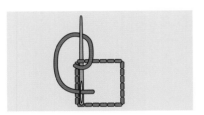

3 Insert the needle from below under the left-most back stitch on the top edge. Wrap the needle in an anticlockwise direction.

❶ *Only enter the fabric at the ends of the rows.*

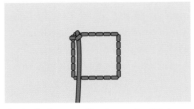

4 Pull the needle through. Tighten by pulling the thread down, until there is a neat knot.

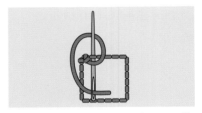

5 From below, insert the needle under the next back stitch. Wrap the needle in an anticlockwise direction.

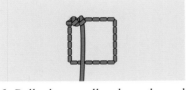

6 Pull the needle through and down, to create another small knot.

7 Continue working a knot in each back stitch to the end of the row. Take the thread to the back on the outside of the backstitch.

8 At the same edge, bring the needle out on the outside of the back stitching, level with the gap between the first and second back stitches.

9 Insert the needle under the thread between the closest two knots. Wrap the needle in a clockwise direction.

10 Pull the needle through and down, tightening to create a small knot.

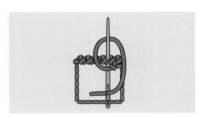

11 Insert the needle under the thread between the next two knots. Wrap the needle in a clockwise direction.

12 Work a knot between each of the previous row's knots. Take the thread to the back outside the outline.

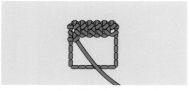

13 Bring the thread out at the top of the third back stitch on the left side. Work a knot before the end one in the previous row.

14 Work a knot between each of the previous row's knots. Finish with a knot after the last one in the previous row. Take the thread to the back outside the outline.

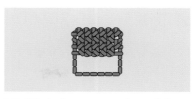

15 Work the next row from right to left, with knots between each of the knots in the previous row.

16 Working from left to right, with knots between each of the previous row's knots and also one extra at each end of the row.

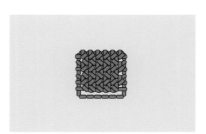

17 Work the next row from right to left, with knots between each of the knots in the previous row.

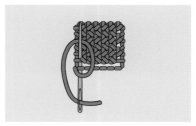

18 For the last row, insert the needle under the first back stitch and the thread at the end of the previous row. Take the thread across and right behind the needle point.
❶ *Do not enter the fabric.*

19 Pull the needle through and down, tightening to create a small knot.

20 Continue in the same way to complete the row. Take the thread to the back at the far side of the back stitching.

❶ *Threads must be started and finished at the ends of rows – not in the middle. If there is not have enough thread to make it to the end of the row, finish the thread off at the end of the previous row. Start the new thread at the beginning of the next row. Fasten off threads in the back of stitching.*
❶ *Left-handers use the same method for trellis stitch as is shown here.*

increasing and decreasing

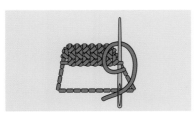

To increase at the ends of a row, insert extra stitches before the closest knot of the previous row, where necessary.

To decrease at the ends of a row, do not work any extra stitches before the first knot of the previous row, as necessary, thereby gradually decreasing the number of stitches per row.

colour shading

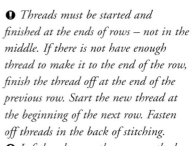

❶ *Different thread colours can be introduced for new rows, to create shading effects. Make sure the outlining matches the colour used for the trellis stitch.*

spiral trellis stitch

Spiral trellis stitch creates textured button-like circles.

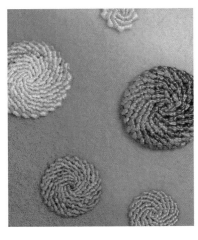

1 Outline the circle in short back stitches.

2 Using a tapestry needle, bring the thread out just inside the back stitching. From below, insert the needle under the stitch just right of the emerging thread. Wrap the needle in an anticlockwise direction.

❶ *Do not enter the fabric at any point.*

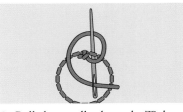

3 Pull the needle through. Tighten by pulling the thread down, until there is a neat knot. Moving in a clockwise direction, insert the needle under the next backstitch. Wrap the needle in an anticlockwise direction.

4 Continue working a knot in each of the back stitches, until the stitching meets the beginning.

❶ *Turn the work as necessary to assist with easy insertion of the needle.*

5 Upon meeting the first stitch, instead of working into each backstitch, work knots into the thread between each of the previous knots.

6 Continue working rounds until the stitches start to become a little crowded as you get closer to the centre.

❶ *It is difficult to join new threads as there are no obvious anchor points. Tie the old and new threads together with a small, secure, neat knot as close to the stitching as possible. Trim the ends, then push it to the back of the stitching between the knots. Continue stitching.*

7 Work a round to decrease the quantity of stitches by skipping stitches e.g. work two knots, then skip a stitch.

❶ *For larger circles, the decreasing will need to be more gradual, so between rows of decreasing, you will need to work non-decreasing rounds where there is a stitch between each knot. When the stitches become crowded again, work another decreasing round.*

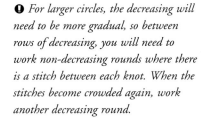

8 Continue on, decreasing periodically, and as the stitches become overcrowded again, nearer the centre, decrease more sharply e.g. work a knot, then skip a stitch.

9 On reaching the centre, take the thread through to the back and secure.

❶ *Left-handers use the same method as is shown here.*

turkey work

Also known as *Ghiordes knot*, this stitch is a tufted stitch that creates a plush pile when worked closely. It is created with overlapping stitches that are alternately pulled tight or left looped.

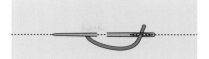

1 Use one guide. Bring the thread out on the line. A little way to the right, insert the needle in the line, bringing it out again halfway back. Keep the thread below the needle.

2 Pull the needle through, so that the stitch sits flat on the fabric.

3 Using the same distance as before, insert the needle further along the line. Bring the needle out at the end of the previous stitch. Keep the thread above the needle.

4 Pull the needle through so that the stitch stays sitting up in a tall loop.
❶ *The length of the loop will determine the length of the cut pile.*

5 Using the same distance as before, insert the needle further along the line. Bring it out again at the end of the previous stitch. Keep the thread below the needle.

6 Pull the needle through, so that the stitch sits flat on the fabric.

7 Using the same distance as before, insert the needle further along the line. Bring the needle out at the end of the previous stitch. Keep the thread above the needle.

8 Pull the needle through so that the stitch stays sitting up in a tall loop.
❶ *Subsequent loops should be the same length as the first looped stitch.*

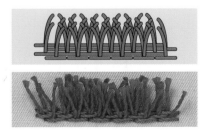

9 Continue in the same manner to build up a line of stitching.

10 Work another row of stitching in front of the previous row, from left to right. Start half a stitch length right of the previous row.

11 Work additional lines of stitching, to fill the required space, with every second line offset by half a stitch length.

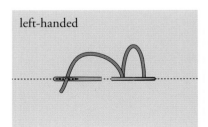

12 Using sharp scissors, cut all the loops, and trim them so that they are all the same desired length.

left-handed

❶ *Left-handers work in mirror image, from right to left.*

vandyke stitch

This stitch is very similar to Ceylon stitch and ladder stitch. Vandyke has one plait down the centre, whereas they have two or more plaits anywhere across the span.

1 Use two vertical guide lines. Bring the thread out on the left line. A little above that, make a short stitch from right to left, centrally between the two lines.

2 Pull the needle through. Insert the needle in the right line, level with where the thread first emerged. Bring it out on the left line a little below the first stitch.

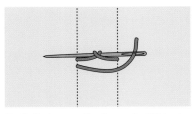

3 Pull the needle through. Slide the needle from right to left under the crossed threads in the centre.
❶ *Do not enter the fabric.*

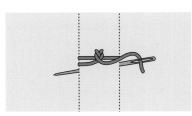

4 Insert the needle in the right line, level with where the thread last emerged. Bring it out on the left line just below the previous stitch.

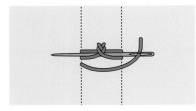

5 Pull the needle through. Slide the needle from right to left under the lowest crossed threads in the centre.
❶ *Do not enter the fabric.*

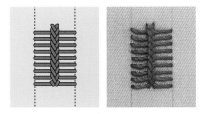

6 Continue in the same manner to build up a line of stitches. Anchor the final stitches with a short stitch on either side of the central plait.

left-handed

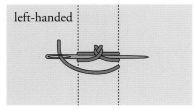

❶ *For left-handers, this stitch is worked in mirror image.*

wheat ear stitch

This stitch is usually worked in straight lines, but can also be used on gentle curves.

1 Use three guides. Bring the thread out on the right line. Insert the needle, a little way below, in the centre line. Bring the needle out on the left line, level with the first stitch's top.

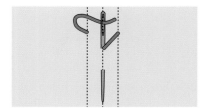

2 Pull the needle through. Insert the needle into the centre line at the bottom of the first stitch. Bring the needle out again a short way below.

3 Pull the needle through. Slide the needle under the previous two stitches, from right to left.
❶ *Do not enter the fabric.*

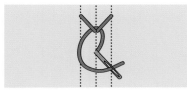

4 Take the thread through to the back, on the line, where the thread emerged.

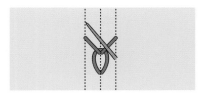

5 Using the same spacing as for the first wheat ear, bring the needle out on the right line.

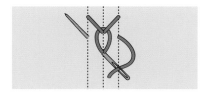

6 Insert the needle at the base of the first wheat ear. Bring it out on the left line level with the top of the previous stitch.

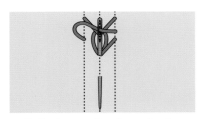

7 Pull the needle through. Insert the needle into the centre line at the bottom of the previous stitch. Bring the needle out again on the middle line, using the same spacing as before.

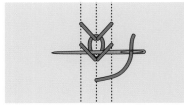

8 Pull the needle through. Slide the needle under the two diagonal stitches, from right to left.
❶ *Do not enter the fabric.*
❶ *Do not take the needle under the chain section.*

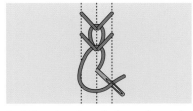

9 Take the thread through to the back, on the line, where the thread emerged.

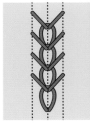 

10 Continue in the same way to build up a line of stitches.

❶ *Wheat ears can also be used singly.*

left-handed

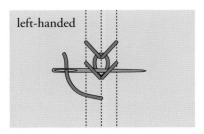

❶ *Left-handers work this stitch in mirror image.*

woven picot

This method is used to create large picots. They can be worked on the surface of the fabric, as shown, or on an edge, or a woven or buttonholed bar.

1 Bring the thread out of the fabric. Just right of it, insert a pin in the fabric so that it emerges level with the thread.

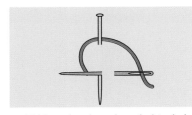

2 Taking the thread up behind the head of the pin, insert the needle on the other side of the pin, using the same spacing as before. Bring the needle out at the pin.

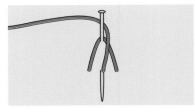

3 Pull the needle through and take the thread up behind the head of the pin, from right to left.

4 Turn the work 90 degrees anticlockwise. From below, slide the needle under the bottom thread, over the middle one, and under the top one.
❶ *Do not enter the fabric at any stage during the weaving.*

5 Pull the needle through and upwards, and to the left to tighten the threads around the pin.

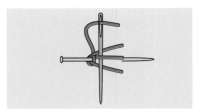

6 From above, slide the needle under the middle thread.

7 Pull the needle through. From below, take the needle under the bottom thread, over the middle and under the top one.

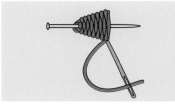

8 Continue weaving back and forth. When the picot is full, take the thread to the back at the base of the picot.

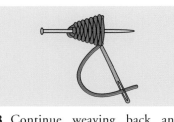

9 Remove the pin and turn the work 90 degrees clockwise for the final effect.

left-handed

❶ *Left-handers work this stitch in mirror image.*

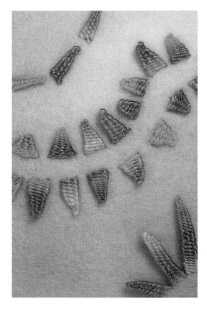

index